Collected Masonic Papers

2012 Transactions
of the
Louisiana Lodge of Research

Collected Masonic Papers

2012 Transactions of the Louisiana Lodge of Research

Published by the Louisiana Lodge of Research
by agreement with
Cornerstone Book Publishers
Copyright © 2012 by Louisiana Lodge of Research
http://louisianalodgeofresearch.org

Cornerstone Book Publishers
New Orleans, LA
www.cornerstonepublishers.com

ISBN-10: 161342048X
ISBN-13: 978-1-61342-048-5

MADE IN THE USA

Table of Contents

2012 Officers of the Louisiana Lodge of Research

Worshipful Master: MW Clayton J. Borne, III, PGM
Senior Warden: Daniel Castoriano
Junior Warden: Azikiwe K Lombard, MD
Secretary/Treasurer: W. Michael R. Poll, PM
Chaplain: W. Nicholas Auck, PM
Senior Deacon: RW William J. Mollere, GJW
Master Expert: W. Klaus Kueck, PM
Junior Deacon: MW Woody Bilyeu, PGM
Inner Guard: W. Glenn Cupit, PM
Master of Ceremonies: W. Naresh Sharma, PM
Tiler: W. Henry Thibodaux, PM

Past Masters of the Louisiana Lodge of Research

1989-90: William J. Mollere
1991: Ballard L. Smith
1992: Irving I. Berglass
1993: Philip J. Walker, Jr
1994: Beryl C. Franklin
1995: Ernest C. Belmont, Jr
1996: Thomas P. Brown
1997: Larry H. Moore
1998: Darrell L. Aldridge
1999: Edward W. Brabham, Jr
2000: Howard F. Entwistle, Jr
2001: Johnnie K. Hill
2002: Richard L. James
2003: Terrell Howes
2004: Glenn Cupit
2005: Robert Bazzell
2006: John Bellanger
2007: Jimmy Leger
2008: Ion Lazar
2009: Bill Richards
2010: Ricks Bowles
2011: Clayton J. Borne, III

The Grand Lodge of Louisiana, F&AM
P.O. Box 12357
5746 Masonic Drive
Alexandria, Louisiana. 71315-2357
Website: http://www.la-mason.com

M:W: Frank N. duTreil, Jr.
Grand Master
R:W: H. Edward Durham
Deputy Grand Master
R:W: Earl J. "Mickey" Durand
Grand Senior Warden
R:W: William J. Mollere
Grand Junior Warden
M:W: Joseph H. Baker, Jr., P.G.M.
Grand Treasurer
M:W: Roy B. Tuck, Jr., P.G.M.
Grand Secretary

Collected Masonic Papers

x

THE RELEVANCY OF FREEMASONRY
IN THE TWENTY FIRST CENTURY
by Clayton J. Borne, III, P.G.M. (Louisiana)
Worshipful Master, Louisiana Lodge of Research

"What is it about the Masonic Brotherhood that has intrigued men for thousands of years? Do the principles established by our ancient Brothers have any relevancy to the way in which we live our lives today?" To answer this question a cursory historical analysis of the development our Fraternity and its cornerstone principles would be in order.

The disciplines of the Masonic Fraternity have been embraced over the course of history and have been identified with diverse social movements. From ultra-conservatives to utopian socialists all found a moral principle embraced in the teachings of the brotherhood that gave their cause credibility and Universal Appeal. The Masonic movement relentlessly moved for the recognition of the rights of man, the endless battle against blind ignorance, uncompromising intolerance, emotional superstition and human error. But where is the basic common bond in the Universal Brotherhood? What are the basic elements and the fundamental principles that bonded these men of all ages together and formed the basis for a disciplined social order? The more interesting questions, are these principals relevant today?

George Washington, Benjamin Franklin, the Marquis deLafayette and many other historical icons passionately embraced Freemasonry and its moral order, finding gratitude in the honor of having their names included in its numbers. But exactly what were those principles that would create the attraction? Was it the International Alliances made possible by the Brotherhood or was it more fundamental concepts? Considering the historical events in which these men were involved allow us an insight into the concepts that commanded their loyalty. The revolutionary concepts of Liberty, Equality and Fraternity consumed their entire being. They literally guaranteed the success of these social ideals with their lives. The idea of a society built on these principles would create a new social order which would culminate and insure economic and social equality. What possible environment would there have been in the 1700's that would insure the academic freedom that would have permitted the development of these revolutionary concepts with the complete assurance of total secrecy? Could it have been within the sacred halls of their Masonic lodges? To these honored men these principals of Brotherhood were their passion and the idealistic concepts that were to form the foundation for the American and French Revolutions. But were these the cornerstone principles or do we search for more basic concepts?

It is this writer's sincere belief that masonry was and is a philosophy of life which, by definition, transcends the limits of time. Its conscience birth, as in all spiritual movements, must be identified as that moment in time when the Grand Architect of the Universe, our Creator God, gave or developed in early man that unique quality which would separate him from the rest of his creation, a rational conscience. With this gift, man was able to then exercise the spiritual quality of choosing good over evil, and thereby able to render obedience to the will of his Creator. This principle was then, just as today, at the core of the Masonic discipline.

The earliest historical records reflect and confirm for our study numerous ancient societies of virtuous men dedicated to establishing a civilized order in the midst of early man's chaos and barbarianism. The ancient philosopher, Aristotle, discusses this discipline in what is described by modern scholars as "Theories of the Good," and more recently developed by legal scholars as "Classical Republicanism." In brief, Aristotle taught that a good life is a virtuous life, and virtue consists partly in being willing to subordinate one's private end to the common welfare, with man seen as a political being whose happiness and self-realization come only through participation in public life, thereby allowing him to achieve psychic independence and ultimately becoming a responsible citizen.

Originally, these movements in the earliest of times developed within organized societies and their teachings were referred to as the Ancient Mysteries. What were the principles developed in these primitive societies that eventually led to a disciplined social order?

This writer submits that these developing societies were uniquely different for three (3) identifiable reasons. First was their spiritual curiosity particularly into the concept of the oneness of God (Monotheism). Second was the corresponding concept of the spirit life after death (Transubstantiation). These spiritual objectives were reflected in the third reason, namely, their personal development and advancement in science and morality (Transformation).

These characteristics logically created, in addition to the most basic concepts of survival, an identifiable purpose for life. These men shook hands with their souls, and in so doing helped to mold the development of an order in society. Their purpose, which developed into identifiable dogma, was "Unity with God" on earth and in the spirit afterlife or heaven.

Monotheism: The human acceptance and belief in the concept of the oneness of God was slow to gain favor. It embodies the aspiration of the soul toward the absolute and infinite intelligence, namely the one Supreme Deity, God. It was gradual, with the people unwilling to relinquish their guardian deities: Diana, Zeus, Apollo, Hermes, and the most cherished Demeter "Mother Earth;" and her daughter Persephone. They were the embodiment of the Mystery of the Harvest, of which Socrates and Aristotle, and then through Aristotle to Alexander, were initiates.

Transubstantiation: The mystery of transubstantiation refers to the spirit life after death and our ability as mortal being to eventually, upon death, pass to it. In Agres Savill's excellent study on Alexander the Great, she writes of Cicero, reflecting on Demeter, Persephone, and the Mystery of the harvest. The mysteries perceive the real principles of life and learn not only to live happy, but to die with a fair hope."

Transformation: Further, this philosophy or teaching advocates self-transformation, or the development of a character that recognizes the need to subrogate self-interest to the interest of the common welfare. It is the awakening of each man's higher self or his spiritual nature, as opposed to his religious theology, which forms the foundation for individual enlightenment.

Throughout ancient times, these men and their collective activities of pursuing these spiritual objectives formed a fundamental as opposed to an organizational unity. They were bound by and found happiness in an alliance of virtue and common ideals in the development of our order. This alliance was not recognized as an historical event with a distinctive identifiable institution until later during the dawn of the operative era of stone masonry.

These societies were also unique in that they advocated the sacred nature of work, which anthropologists stress is identified in most spiritual, as opposed to religious, movements. Further as an extension of these disciplines, the concept of justice was given birth. Individuals were recognized as having rights based or conditioned upon man's fundamental assumption of the obligations necessary to establish a desired order in society.

These movements, with their dedication and commitment to a Higher Spirituality, preserved, through esoteric instructions, the ancient legends, traditions, charges and disciplines for those of us who would later travel the road of this life's reality. The tracking of the spiritual objectives and traditions of these Ancient Societies is one of the only possible ways to establish a true Genealogy of Freemasonry prior to 925 AD.

It is this writer's sincere belief that the spiritual or mystic core of Freemasonry, based on the principles of transubstantiation and transformation have not essentially changed over the history of mankind. Respected histories document these cornerstone principles and spiritual objectives appearing in diverse cultures and for our study our interest focus on those which later developed as operative artesian societies.

The *Hamitic Egyptians*_(4000 BC) that migrated to all parts of the Mediterranean to be know as the Etruscans in Italy, the Pelasgoi in Greece, and the Hittities in Asia were referred to by historians as the "Temple Builders". The *Zoroastians* (3000 BC) in Persia, the *Rosicrucians* (1500 BC) in Egypt, the *Druids* (1000 BC) and the *Essences* (200 BC) are evidences of spiritually motivated, disciplined societies, all having an artesian component.

This writer is convinced that our fraternity is the result of no one identifiable institution or school of thought, but rather a philosophical and spiritual movement emerging in Ancient Artesian Societies where man is seen individually and collectively confronting his humanness in an attempt to understand himself and his place in the universe. It is the challenge of viewing human existence played out in life by the struggle between the powers of evil relentlessly confronting through temptation the divine principles of good.

The advocacy of an unselfish state of being achieved through a disciplined transformation of one's life was then, just as it is in our fraternity today, encouraged in these societies in order to achieve the ultimate rewards of sharing eternity with one's creator. This philosophy fostered, even in the most ancient times, the principles of character: truth, morality, and brotherly love. As is often stated, the movement fosters a Brotherhood of Man under the Fatherhood of God.

4

This writer further submits that although the core spiritual concepts of transubstantiation and transformation appeared in various unrelated cultures and was not unique to one society, when these core concepts emerged in the teaching of ancient societies of architects and builders, the spark was ignited which would eventually culminate in our Masonic fraternity. It is clear, however that the craft's philosophy and teachings preceded its formal organization by thousands of years. Reaching that point in history which we refer to as the "Operative Period", the alliance or virtue and common ideals had finally developed a distinct identity.

Irrespective of when this spiritual and operative alliance began, the principles of the Masonic Fraternity continue to challenge the brotherhood to elevate the awareness of God in their lives and enhance the family of mankind through implementation of the cornerstone principal of Charity, expressed through Friendship, Morality, and Brotherly Love. Man's implementation of the virtue of "Charity" was then, just as it is now, the passageway through which God bestows His mercies and blessings upon mankind.

The *Dionysian Architects* (1055 BC) with their signs and symbols for recognition purposes combined operative skills while emphasizing as their purpose charity, The *Roman Collegia* (715 BC) were the keepers of the trade secrets of the Roman Empire; the *Euclidian School* (323 BC) evidenced the esoteric traditions of the Liberal Sciences as taught by the Greek geometrician Euclid (323 BC – 283 BC) were all clearly identifiable societies whose dimensions and spiritual objectives clearly mirror very distinctive evidence of the origin of our Brotherhood and its spiritual identity.

Within the confines of these movements, influenced by these social, economic and spiritual development, the Masonic craft walked across the pages of history similar to other trade unions with the major exception of their banding together and allowing their philosophers to be concerned not only with the spiritual nature of their Artisan trades, but with the orderly progress of humanity and a defined social order.

In its daily practice the individual advancement in our craft was achieved by the Master Artisans teaching their initiates to apply the Principles of Operative Masonry and Architecture to the Science and Art of Human Self Awareness and Character Building. It was the development of a system of morality defined in the form of ritual and usually veiled by its masters, teachers, or elders by allegories and symbols. The "Old Changes," found in the Gothic or York Constitutions during the 1300s, confirm that the ancient operatives struggled to preserve this dynamic principle and traditions as found in the crafts' disciplines from Egypt through Jordan into Europe.

This writer further submits that the evolution and development of speculative Freemasonry is noted historically by the formal organization of our fraternity into a formal brotherhood operating under defined constitutions wherein the principles of the order are taught by signs, allegories, charges, and lectures exemplified within the framework of defined degrees, symbolizing advancement in spiritual and moral development. The noted Masonic historian, Mackey attempted to define the fundamental principles governing the modern-day Craft in a twenty-five point list, referred to as the "Landmarks of Freemasonry." The principles, signs and symbols of the modern-day Craft, as in the ancient orders, are still grounded upon the principle of obedience to the will of the grand architect of the universe, our creator, God.

The 21st century presents man with a high tech society which functions completely at the mercy of the computer. We now talk to computers; we allow computers to think for us. The computer has the ability to provide society with all of its needs. It brings the world to our fingertips. All of this is considered an advancement as it makes the complex nature of modern society manageable and efficient. However it has a corresponding negative result in that it creates personal isolationism where there is no need for human contact or personal commitment to anything much less disciplined causes, such as moral, compassionate caring societies, the dynamic elements that our brotherhood has fought to maintain.

This quest in our modern day society is only possible and able to be accomplished through an insistence and reliance on the principle of truth and a defined spiritual objective. It is only in this way that man can have continued spiritual and intellectual growth and continued transformation to improve justice in society with a distinct collective reflection and imprint on the community in which we live.

These changing times present man with the ability to live a very different lifestyle; however our most basic needs as social creatures remain the same. The basic tenets of Truth, Charity and Brotherly Love as espoused by our Spiritual Brotherhood are as necessary to us as individuals as they are to the progression of an ordered society. This is as true today as it was to our ancient brothers. As the brotherhood employs its tenets in its daily lives we are better able to understand why our forefathers embraced the dynamic sociological principles of Liberte', Egalite' and Fraternite' as espoused in our brotherhood. Are these principles relevant in the 21st century? How is it even thinkable they would not? They are essential and it is our brotherhood's mission to insure that they endure.

THE EVOLUTION OF THE THREE GREAT LIGHTS
By John L. Belanger, P.M.
Past Master, Louisiana Lodge of Research

The study of the Evolution of the Three Great Lights in my opinion is a very complex one. To understand this we must start back in time prior to the three great light being placed on our altars in modern (Speculative) masonry. We will now journey into time together and search the background that it may give us a deeper understanding of our Masonic Heritage.

When we were first made a Master Masons we saw the Three Great Lights (Holy Bible, Square and Compass) and thought that all of our fore fathers (Operative and Speculative) saw the same on their Masonic Altar. Also most of us thought they always had three degrees in masonry (Entered Apprentice, Fellow Craft, and Master Mason) from its conception. I know I did.

We are taught that Masonry is divided into two denominations:

1. Operative Masonry, which we refer to our ancient brethren that built buildings out of mortar prior to 1717; example a square is used to square a building or corners , etc.

2. while Speculative Masonry, which started around 1717, use the same tools however, we used them in a more practical purpose of life; example the square teaches us to square our actions by the square of virtue, etc. With this in mind let us begin our journey.

The search will begin in the 1600's with the operative masonry, our heritage. The Guild of Operative Free Masons whose ceremonies the Society wishes to recall and reflect is the Fylfot Cross or better know since World War II as the swastika. This was *long before* Hitler hijacked the swastika emblem and turned it into the emblem of hatred which many regard it as today. The Operatives used to have a large white swastika (*Fylfot Cross*), about two feet by two feet, on the floor of their Assemblages, another on the open Bible, at various points they included them in their ceremonies, and some would occasionally show them after their names, like a sort of mason's mark. It was, they claimed, the Master Mason's Talisman, its history could be traced for centuries, and it was central to their ceremonies.

Both Clement Stretton and Dr. Carr claimed that the swastika is probably the most ancient and widely distributed symbol that has ever existed, tracing its origin to the masons of the Turanians who are said to have lived before the Babylonian Empire and to have carried their craft from central Asia to China, India and Tibet, so that "it has been found on Chaldean bricks; among the ruins of Troy; in Egypt; on the vases and pottery of ancient Cyprus; on prehistoric antiquities of Greece and Mycenae; on the vases and pottery of the ancient Etruscans; on Hittite remains; on rock walls of Buddhist cave temples in India; in China and Japan; in prehistoric American Indian mounds; on prehistoric remains in Central America and South America. In later or historic times it has been found on Roman altars; on Runic monuments in Great Britain; on Gothic and Scandinavian weapons and ornaments; in the Coptic Church of the Xth Century; on English brasses of the XIIIth and XIVth Centuries, as well as many other parts of Europe"(Carr, 1910) and it is still *displayed on the flag of the Jains of India today.* In Britain it is known as the Fylfot Cross.

It seems that the ancients adopted the swastika as a symbol of the axial rotation of the Big Dipper (sometimes referred to as Ursa Major or the Plough) around the Pole Star which, in turn, they regarded as a symbol of God himself because, in the constantly changing heavens, only the Pole Star remained constant whilst all other stars revolved around it. A Pole Star cult, it will be remembered, long preceded the Solar Cult with which we are more familiar today.

Carr explained that when a new 3rd Master Mason was appointed within the Guild, he was taken to an underground chamber below the central column, and told to raise his eyes to heaven, looking up a plumb-line dropped from the Temple roof, through the lodge, into the chamber below. At the top of that plumb-line he would see "the Star of Heaven, the Pole Star, the 'I am'. the 'G' in the roof" which he was ordered to worship." Each limb of the swastika apparently represented a different Hebrew letter, so that the whole symbol was not just a *symbol* of El Shaddai, it represented the Holy Name itself.

Today's Operatives, therefore, simply adopted the sign because it was so highly regarded by the Guild masons they wish to recall but, apart from displaying it on their Bibles, they have now curtailed its use out of respect for the sensitivities of those who suffered at the hands of the Nazis. They merely put a small swastika (Fylfot Cross) on the Bible at the opening of the Assemblage, because - according to Clement Edwin Stretton and John Yarker - who were writing at the turn of the 20th century (i.e. around 1900), that is what the ancient Free Masons did in their Assemblages. They claimed that the swastika was so important to the old operatives, that they used to display a large one on the floor of their lodges. Moreover, on certain occasions, the workmen formed themselves into four gammadions (i.e.each arm of which was shaped like an 'L') with 8 men making-up each arm. The important thing is that, at the time they were writing, there was nothing sinister about the swastika. It has been used for thousands of years and, like the Hindoos and Jains, they simply regarded it as a sort of Heavenly symbol of good fortune, which represented the movement of certain planets around the Pole Star. Adolf Hitler changed all that by adopting the swastika as the symbol of the National Socialist Party, and ever since the late 1930s (and the 2nd World War) it has been regarded as a sign of something evil. **For your information, Fylfot Crosses can be found in virtually every Cathedral (and many churches) in England**. It has only been a hated symbol (by some) since the 2nd World War. Because of that, and the fact that so many people are understandably 'sensitive' about its use, the modern Operatives no longer place a Fylfot Cross on the floor, and we do not form 32 men into a swastika. The Worshipful Deputy Master, **Super Intendent of Work,** and the two Deputies (Deputy Jackin & Deputy Boaz) simply (and quietly) form a small swastika on the top of the Bible to reflect the importance of that symbol to the Ancient masons. Remember, the whole purpose of the modern Operative Society is to perpetuate a memorial of the practices of the ancient Guild masons from whom (we believe) modern freemasonry is descended.

The following extract, however, from F. W. Seal-Coon's account of the Guild's 'Midsummer Ceremony' is given to illustrate the Guild's use of the swastika. The events described occur immediately after five 'sacrifices' (from amongst "those without blemish") have been symbolically slain:

"Following the sacrifice, thirty-two brethren form a Gammadion, a figure formed of four mason's squares (also known as a 'fylfot' or 'swastika'). The squares of the mosaic pavement of an operative lodge were a sacred cubit(21 7/8 inches) in area and on these squares the masons, eight to each arm, formed the Gammadion; the thirty-third square at the centre, under the symbol of the Pole Star from which hung a plumb-line, was left empty."

"Christian freemasons will have no problem interpreting the number thirty-three, which is just one of the reasons why I hope the Society never abandons the sign completely. Another is that I am personally reluctant to allow something evil, which lasted for only a comparatively short time, to end a tradition which is said to have existed for centuries. Originally, the swastika was a good luck sign and the word itself was derived from the Sanskrit *svastika* - 'su' meaning 'good', 'asti' meaning 'to be', and 'ka' as a suffix. I prefer to think of it that way."

Creation of the First Grand Lodge in London (Speculative Masonry begins)

Since Speculative Freemasonry Masonry started in England around 1717, there has been no mention of the *Fylfot Cross* being used at any time in the Masonic Lodges.

English Masonic historians place great importance on June 24, 1717, (St. John the Baptist's day) when four London lodges came together at the Goose and Gridiron Ale House in St Paul's churchyard and formed what they called The Grand Lodge of England. Although Freemasonry had existed in England since at least the mid-17th century and in Scotland since The Schaw Statutes were enacted in 1598 and 1599, the establishment of a permanent Grand Lodge in London in 1717 is traditionally considered the formation of organized Freemasonry in its modern sense. We must remember that they only had two degrees at that time referred to as the 1st and 2nd. When a brother received the 1st, he was considered a full brother mason and went to all meetings paying dues.

Creation of the Third Degree

Sometime after 1725, a third degree, the Master Mason's degree, began to be worked in London lodges. Its origins are unknown. While it may be older than its recorded appearance indicates, it does not appear in the records of any lodge until April 1727 (its actual conferral does not appear in the records of any lodge until March 1729). Exposures of Masonic ritual, which began to appear in 1723, refer to only two degrees until the publication of Samuel Pritchard's "Masonry Dissected" in 1730, which contained the work for all three degrees. The Master Mason's degree was not official until the Grand Lodge adopted Anderson's revised Constitutions of 1738.

The "Antients'" and "Moderns" Grand Lodges

Throughout the early years of the new Grand Lodge, there were many lodges that never affiliated with the new Grand Lodge. These unaffiliated Masons and their Lodges were referred to as "Old Masons," or "St. John Masons, and "St. John Lodges".

In 1725, a lodge in York founded the rival "Grand Lodge of All England" as a protest against the growing influence of the Grand Lodge of England in London. During the 1730s and 1740s, antipathy increased between the London based Grand Lodge of England (hereafter referred to as the Premier Grand Lodge) and the Grand Lodges of Ireland and Scotland. Irish and Scots Masons visiting and living in London considered the Premier Grand Lodge to have considerably deviated from the ancient practices of the Craft. As a result, these Masons felt a stronger kinship with the unaffiliated London Lodges. The aristocratic nature of the Premier Grand Lodge and its members alienated other Masons of the City causing them also to identify with the unaffiliated Lodges.

On July 17, 1751, representatives of five Lodges gathered at the Turk's Head Tavern, in Greek Street, Soho, London — forming a rival Grand Lodge — The Most Antient and Honourable Society of Free and Accepted Masons. They believed that they practiced a more ancient and therefore purer form of Masonry, and called their Grand Lodge *The Antients' Grand Lodge*. They called those affiliated to the Premier Grand Lodge, by the pejorative epithet *The Moderns*. These two unofficial names stuck. Laurence Dermott wrote a new constitution for the Ancients, the Ahiman Rezon as an alternative for the Constitution of the *Moderns*.

An illustration of how deep the division was between the two factions is the case of Benjamin Franklin who was a member of a Moderns' Lodge in Philadelphia. During his stay in France, he became Master of the Lodge Les Neuf Sœurs in 1779, and was re-elected in 1780. Upon returning from France, it transpired that his Lodge had changed to (and had received a new warrant from) the Antients Grand Lodge; no longer recognizing him and declining to give him "Masonic Honours" at his funeral.

For many years, "The Great Masonic Schism" was a name applied to the sixty-two year division of English Freemasonry into two separate Grand Lodges. Some even attempted to attribute the division to the changes in passwords made in 1738–39 by the Premier

Grand Lodge. Masonic historian Robert F. Gould in his "History of Freemasonry (1885) referred to the Antients Grand Lodge as "schismatics". However, Henry Sadler, Librarian of the UGLE, demonstrated in his 1887 book "Masonic Facts and Fictions" that the Antients Grand Lodge was formed in 1751 primarily by Irish Masons living and working in London, never affiliated with the older Grand Lodge. 72 of the first 100 names on the roll of the new Antients' Grand Lodge were Irish. In 1776, the Grand Secretary of the Moderns' Grand Lodge referred to them as "the Irish Faction (Ye Antient Masons, as they call themselves)". And so the myth of a "Great Masonic Schism" in English Masonry was laid to rest.

Grand Lodges founded during the Colonial Era

Freemasonry spread from the British Isles during the Colonial Era. All of the "original" Grand Lodges began to issue charters to individual lodges in North America, but the two English Grand Lodges (the "Ancients" and the "Moderns") were the most prolific. Starting in 1730, The Grand Lodge of England (Moderns) began to issue Warrants for Provincial Grand Lodges in the colonies. Initially, these Warrants were issued to individuals, to act as deputies for the Grand Master in a given area for fixed periods of time, and some confusion resulted due to overlapping jurisdictions. To confuse matters further, with the formation of the Ancient Grand Lodge, rival Provincial Grand Lodges were chartered under their jurisdiction.

Independent Grand Lodges

After the American Revolution and the incorporation of the Dominion of Canada, the various Provincial Grand Lodges in North America were closed, and the Lodges in each State or Province formed independent Grand Lodges. These in turn, chartered lodges in the territories in the West and North. As each new State or Province came into being, the lodges that had been chartered within its borders gathered together and formed new Grand Lodges.

Talking to P.G.M. Edward O. Weisser, of Pennsylvania, who stated "In 1731 the Grand Master received the Master Mason Degree only. Most men only received the EA and maybe the FC. This is why, at the end of the EA degree, the candidate is told "now we may call you brother". Later, it seems to have been decided that each worshipful master had to have earned/received the Master Masons Degree. The Grand Lodge of Pennsylvania in 1731 was called Modern and in 1820 became Ancient which at that time or around then the Master Mason Degree was then it was extended to everyone; thus now, one is not a "full" brother until he has received the Master Mason Degree." This information was found in the Grand Lodge of Pennsylvania proceedings.

The Square and Compass (In Kennings Cyclopaedia of Freemasonry, dated 1878) states:

Compass: "A Masonic emblem too well known to need elaboration here, and adhering to our principle, we restrain ourselves from higher tendency of ritualistic explanation."

Square: "One of the most important and significant of Masonic symbols. It is often seen in churches, as an emblem of the old operative builders, and is no doubt of very early use. Upon the very early metal square found in Ireland near Limerick, these words, dated 1517,

I will strive to live with ease and care,
Upon the level, by the square.

If this is the operative teaching of 1517, it, of course points to mediaeval teaching, akin to present speculative application of the working tools of the operative mason."

In Volume 82 (1969) of Ars Quatuor Coronatorum (i.e. the Transactions of Quatuor Coronati Lodge No. 2076 and can be found on pp 327-8. It concerns "Square, Compass and the Points", and is an answer provided by the Editor of the Transactions in the 'Notes and Queries' Section. It reads as follows:

"The earliest description of the 'points' procedure made its appearance in 1760 in an English exposure (Three Distinct Knocks) which claimed to describe the practices of the Masons under the 'Antients' Grand Lodge. It is known that this (and other English exposures of the 1760s) betrayed evidence of French influence, and if TDK was indeed describing 'Antients' practice it probably represented some Irish practices, too. For these reasons, it must be noted that the origins of the procedures cannot definitely be ascribed to any particular country, though we may be reasonably certain that they were current in England - not necessarily widespread - from 1760 onwards. The relevant extract is quoted below, without comment:-The Master always sits in the East, or stands with the Bible before him; and if it is the Apprentice Lecture, he opens it about the Second Epistle of Peter, with the Compass laid thereon, and the Points of them covered with a little Box Square or Lignum Vita, about 4 inches each way, and the Points of the Compass points to the West, and the Two Points of the Square points to the East. If it is the Craft's Lecture, the Master shows one Point of the Compass, the Bible being open at the 12th Chapter of Judges. If it is the Master's Lecture, the Bible is opened about the Seventh Chapter of the First Book of Kings, and both the Points of the Compass is shown upon the Square."

As far as when and where freemasons in England first started to display the Square and Compass on the Bible, in the 'Masonic Trowel', an on-line Masonic website, which states that it could not have been before 1535 (because that is when the first complete Bible in English was published in Britain). Before that, operative masons used to take their Obligation on a copy of the Ancient Charges, the oldest of which (the Regius Manual Script) dates from 1390."

According to the Colne Manual Script No. 1, the first time a bible was used was in 1685, and the relevant instructions states that one of the candidates should lay his right hand upon it when the Charge shall be read. (According to the Edinburgh Register Manual Script of 1696, they did the same thing in Scotland).

In Samuel Prichard's exposure ("Masonry Dissected") of 1730 it describes taking an Obligation ".....my naked Right Hand on the Holy Bible; there I took the Obligation (or oath) of a Mason."

After 1730, "A little later we find the Bible, Square and Compass described as Pillars of the Lodge. The first known reference to Great Lights is to be found in France in 1745 but this meant what are now called Lesser Lights. The first reference to the Bible, Square and Compass as the Three Great Lights appears in English writings about 1760, and this usage was confirmed by the Lodge of Reconciliation set up in the early 1800's to settle differences of practice at the time of the formation of the United Grand Lodge of England."

In Kennings Cyclopaedia of Freemasonry, dated 1878, it explains (on page 603): "Square and Compass":

"A well-known Masonic emblem, and which may often be seen on the great buildings which were raised by the operative masons. It is idle, we think, to suppose that they are of 1717 use, when much evidence might be adduced, of a far earlier habit, of their familiarity to the operative masons and others."

It is certainly long before 1717, and the square and compass (separately, i.e. not as we put them on the bible these days) are both shown on the Society's Coat of Arms, which date from the 15th century, which proves that the operatives were costumed to using them. They're hard to see, but they are laying on top of the chevrons on the two left-hand 'quartering's' of the Operatives current Coat of Arms, the original of which is displayed in the Guild Hall in Durham.

Knowing how masonry evolved from time in Memorial till now we have a better understand where we came from. The questions of when, how, and where the Square, Compass and Holy Bible came to play in Masonry have been answered.

Now, this journey has given us more light in Masonry however, we cannot stop here. We must now take it to a higher level. Our own Grand Lodge has the Fellow Craft emblem on the Louisiana Grand Lodge Seal and all regular documents. However, we have learned that our Grand Lodge Seal on the Grand Lodge proceedings is now the Master Masons emblem within the seal rather than the Fellow Craft emblem.

To understand Louisiana Masonry we must understand the following questions: Why does the Louisiana seal have the Fellow Craft emblem on it? Was it our first and only seal for Louisiana? When and why was it changed on the Grand Lodge proceedings? When our Grand Lodge was first constituted were we conferring all three degrees, if not why? Lastly, which degree were we first opening our Masonic Lodges and conducting regular business in? Was it the Entered Apprentice, Fellow Craft, or Master Mason degree?

My brothers, we have learned in this paper and lots of other Masonic papers that every time we think we understand all of Masonry, another door will open with more information. In our next journey, we will search for these answers from within the Grand Lodge, Masons in Louisiana and various other lodges to possibly bring our search to a conclusion. Until then my brothers, until then. *God Bless you*.

Information obtained from and Additional readings

The Worshipful Society of Free Masons, Rough Masons, Wallers, Slaters, Paviors, Plaisterers and Bricklayers dated 2006) by David Kibble-Rees, 2nd Grand Master of the Operatives in England
David Kibble-Rees, 2nd Grand Master of the Operatives in England- who gave me a lot of insight into European Masonry and for without him this paper could not have been written
Carr, T. - *Operative Free Masons and Operative Free Masonry* (1910).
Seal-Coon, F. - *An Old-Time Operative Midsummer Ceremony*, in AQC, Vol. 105 (1992), pp. 161-171.
Stretton, C. E. Guild Masonry, in the *Transactions* of the Lodge of Research No. 2429 (1910)
Kennings Cyclopaedia of Freemasonry, dated 1878
The Masonic Trowel (several Masonic talks) including "The Volume of the Sacred Law" & "The Philosophy of Freemasonry"
Masonic Education Course the European Concept by Kent Henderson and Tony Pahl
Freemasonry and Social England in the Eighteenth Century by W.B. Gilbert W. Daynes
Samuel Pritchard - *Masonry Dissected* in 1730
Charles H. Merz - *Guild Masonry in the Making* (1918)

THE STORY OF LOUISIANA LODGE OF RESEARCH
by William J. Mollere, G.J.W. (Louisiana)
Past Master, Louisiana Lodge of Research

It was a hot summer day in July 1982, at the Baton Rouge High Twelve luncheon where I finally had the courage to ask R:W: Ray W. Burgess, Grand Junior Warden of the Most Worshipful Grand Lodge of the State of Louisiana, Free and Accepted Masons, the questions that had been whirling around in my mind for two weeks. "Brother Burgess, why doesn't Louisiana have a Research Lodge and why don't we allow Class Lodges?" Bro. Burgess looked over at me, took a deep breath and pointed that expressive finger at my chest and replied, "You obviously know the answer to those questions already, why don't you tell me."

The question of Class Lodges and groups such as Table Lodges were reserved for another period of discussion and debate, but the idea of a Research Lodge became a quest for answers.

Thus began a three-year discussion on the merits of developing a forum where Masons could have a point of focus for scholarly talks on philosophy, esoteric doctrine, history, and heritage. Whenever we could get together and talk about the need and worth of a Research Lodge, Bro. Burgess guided and moulded my thoughts on such an organization. When the time came for him to be elevated to Grand Master in 1985, and lead the Grand Lodge, Bro. Burgess appointed a "Committee to Study the Feasibility of Organizing a Lodge of Research" and named me Chairman, and my long-time friend, Brother Ballard Lee Smith, Vice-Chairman. Bro. Smith had long shared a love of Masonic research and Masonic book collecting. His library and Masonic jewelry collections are very select and probably priceless. Bro. Smith, who is an accountant and CPA by training and vocation, worked to draft the first set of by-laws while, I had the pleasant task of writing to all of the other Research Lodges in the country requesting information. The Southern California and the Southern Arizona Lodges initially supplied a great deal of information. The Texas Lodge of Research supplied the most helpful material. It was almost as if Texas wanted to repay Louisiana in forming our Research Lodge as Louisiana had helped Texas organize its Masonry. It was a rewarding experience contacting Masonic research organizations throughout the country. All were helpful and encouraging. "Whatever you need" and "How we can help" were the two most frequent replies. Masonry in action - extending that helping hand of assistance.

The first year the Committee asked the Grand Lodge for acceptance of a structure - a lodge without the rights of conferral of degrees or duty to pay assessments to the Grand Lodge. The second year saw the report of by-laws and officer arrangement. The third year saw the report to organize and charter. Each year the Grand Lodge enthusiastically supported the concept of a Research Lodge, so no opposition was expected. The third year something incredible happened - the vote of the Grand Lodge was "NO" on formation.

Bro. Smith and I could not believe what we had heard. A "no vote" for a Research Lodge was a vote against motherhood, apple pie, the American way. It was Bro. Burgess who again came over with the steady, seasoned hand. Although he was shaking his head in disbelief, too, he said that some bad information had been circulated. Many of the delegates had been led to believe that the Research Lodge would be an "Inspector General" office for the Grand Lodge. People would come around to check on things and report back to the Grand Master. There was the idea, too, that such a Research Lodge would cost the Grand Lodge money - at a time when there was a budget crisis in every aspect of Louisiana Masonry. Brother Ray's advice was just like the song, "pick yourself up, dust yourself off and start all over again." We did. We went back to the trestleboard and studied our design.

At the next Grand Lodge session, 1989 in Baton Rouge, the Committee was ready. It had done its homework - talked to the District Deputy Grand Masters, Lodge officers, general membership, as many as we could talk to and explain the purposes. The vote was taken on the formation and chartering - unanimous! The new Grand Master, Most Worshipful Eugene Love, was a Masonic researcher in his own right and he wanted the Research Lodge chartered as soon as possible.

He allowed the newly created Research Lodge to solicit members from across the state. At one Grand Lodge Workshop in Baton Rouge in April 1989, the Grand Master announced that he was going to be the first to pay his dues in the new Research Lodge. Immediately 78 people stepped forward and gave their ten dollars for charter membership. The rush was so fast and furious that only 70 names were recorded that day - but there was money for 78! We did not find out who the other eight were!

The Installation of Officers in September, 1989 on Labor Day weekend is a shining day. To realize an idea that began in July, 1982 finally become a Lodge of Research was a magic moment. To have my brother Ballard Lee Smith in the West was a great pleasure. To have Most Worshipful Ray W. Burgess as the Installing Officer was a great honor. Something had been accomplished. It was not always easy, it was measured and studied. It was the Masonic way.

So mote it be.

A VERY BRIEF HISTORY OF THE GRAND LODGE OF FRANCE FROM ITS ORIGINS TO PRESENT TIME

by Daniel Castoriano
Senior Warden, Louisiana Lodge of Research

Introduction

Before one studies the history of any important Grand Lodge (such as the Grand Lodge of France), it is vital to understand the historical, political and philosophical context in which the Grand Lodge was born.

The period surrounding the creation of Grand Lodge of France has been subsequently named the "Age of Enlightenment."[1] This was a cultural movement of intellectuals in the 18th century that sought to develop the power of reason, promoted science, progressive literature[2] and cultural exchanges; it further opposed the intolerance and abuses of the State and of the Church and fought against superstition.[3]

This movement originated in France and spread across Europe to England and Scotland, reaching as far as Russia and Spain and influencing monarchs such as Frederic II of Prussia[4] and Catherine the Great of Russia[5] who became known as "enlightened despots." From Europe, it crossed the Atlantic where it influenced American Revolutionary patriots such as Benjamin Franklin and Thomas Jefferson among many others.

The political ideals of this "Age of Reason" influenced the American *Declaration of Independence* as well as the French *Declaration of the Rights of Man and the Citizen* as well as other progressive Constitutions in Europe.

Origins

The first Grand Lodge of France appears to have been created around the month of July 1728 by Philip, Duke of Wharton, PGM of the Grand Lodge of London, even though operative masons were known to have formed lodges long before this time during the medieval construction of the Cathedrals. Many of these lodges were believed to have been placed under the protection of the Knights Templar.

In 1738, the first French Grand Master was Louis de Pardaillan de Gondrin (1707-1743), 2nd Duke of Antin (Duc d'Antin). The Grand Lodge of France grew rapidly — and, by 1771, there were 41 Lodges in Paris, 169 Lodges in the French provinces, 11 in the French colonies and 5 in foreign countries. In addition there were 31 Lodges for senior military officers.

From the beginning in Freemasonry, noblemen and bourgeoisie rubbed shoulders and exchanged intellectual views.

The French Revolution,[6] which exploded the political system which had been in place in France for more than 200 years, brought about the break-up of the Grand Lodge of France and the creation of the Grand Orient of France — which was created in 1773.

The turmoil of the French Revolution did not spare Masons and, many Lodges disappeared in the maelstrom.

On September 2, 1804 , the Supreme Council of the Ancient and Accepted Rite was created in France by Alexandre Francois Auguste Count de Grasse-Tilly (1765-1845)[7]

At the end of the French Revolution period, Napoleon Bonaparte[8] had become Emperor of France. He ordered all Jurisdictions to merge with the Grand Orient de France, where he had named his brother Louis Bonaparte as Deputy Grand Master the previous year (1803) and Joseph Bonaparte in 1805 as its Grand Master.

On December 5, 1804, a Masonic agreement (Concordat Maconnique)[9] was signed between the Grande Loge Generale Ecossaise, which had been created on September 22, 1804, and the Grand Orient de France.

However, some Lodges refused this political intervention and sought refuge with the Supreme Council of France which had remained independent and had kept its jurisdiction over Scottish Rite craft and higher degrees (the complete 33 degrees of the AASR).

The year 1894 saw the creation of the Grande Loge Symbolique Ecossaise.[10] The Act of 1901 (ratified in 1904) saw the Constitution of the present day Grand Lodge of France.[11]

Outlawed during World War II until Liberation in 1945,[12] the Grand Lodge of France experienced the worst period in its history. Masons from all jurisdictions were persecuted by the Nazi Vichy government and the German occupying forces of WWII.

The Grand Lodge of France today.[13]

There are approximately 31,000 members in 810 Lodges in France and 33 Lodges outside France. Only men are allowed.

The Grand Lodge of France, a sovereign and independent grand lodge, is presided over by the Grand Master, who is elected from the members of a Federal Council through deputies designated by the individual lodges.

The Grand Lodge of France functions in the first 3 degrees of the Ancient and Accepted Scottish Rites of which there are 33 degrees.

In all its works, the Grand Lodge invokes the Grand Architect of the Universe, as the symbolic expression of the Deity or Creator principle of each member of the lodge.

The Declaration of Principles of the Grand Lodge of France.[14]

Article I: The Grand Lodge of France works to the Greater Glory of the Grand Architect of the Universe.

Article II: There are three great lights in the lodge , and on the Altar there must be the Book of the Sacred Law (the Bible), though other Sacred Books (Torah, Q'uran, etc..) are allowed for the first obligation only during the initiation. The Bible is open at the first page of Saint John's Gospel whereupon rests the square and compass.

Article III: Allegiance to the Nation and respect of its institutions and its laws.

Article IV: Prohibits the lodges to involve themselves in any political or religious matters, but individuals are free to adopt any political stance so long as it is not contrary to the principles of the Masonic Order.

Each Freemason of the Grand Lodge of France is totally free as far as religious issues are concerned but must, as a core duty, offer respect for the religious convictions of his brethren.

Conclusion

Today, the Grand Lodge of France is a vibrant and active Masonic organization which respects the Constitutions of Anderson — It focuses and maintains its Masonic traditions. Each lodge works to foster the search of Truth, through the symbolic and intellectual presentations of Freemasonry.

Its Grand Master is Alain-Noel Dubart.
The Grand Lodge of France website is: www.gldf.org
Its address is: 8 rue Puteaux, Paris, France.

Notes & References

(1)-Les Confessions de JJ Rousseau, precede d'une notice par Georges Sand-1841-Private Collection-Castoriano
(2)-Oeuvres de Voltaire -correspondence generale-first edition 1792-Private Collection-Castoriano
(3)-Traite sur la Tolerance-1763-Voltaire (Calas Affair-1761)
(4)-Frederick the Great-King of Prussia-by General Sir David Frasier, GCB, OBE
(5)-Catherine the Great-Henri Troyat-Membre de l'Academie Francaise.
(6)-Institut d'histoire de la revolution francaise /Histoire des francais de Pierre Gaxotte-Membre de l'Academie Francaise.Private Collection-Castoriano
(6)-The French Revolution-Richard Cobb, Professor of modern history at Oxford University, Simon & Schuster 1988-Private Collection-Castoriano
(7) La Franc-Maconnerie dans les colonies francaises sous la revolution francaise-emsomipy.free.fr/
(8)-Napoleon- de Octave Aubry de l'Academie Francaise-1961-Private Collection-Castoriano
(9)-Andre Dore-Le Concordat Maconnique de 1804 et introduction en France du Rite Ecossais Ancien et Accepte-Encyclopoedia Universalis-article Concordat.
(9)-Bibliotheque Nationale-Paris-Fonds Maconnique.
(10) Grande Loge Symbolique Ecossaise ou les avant-gardes maconniques-Francoise Jupeau-Requillard-1998
(11) Act of 1901-Grande Loge de France-Association Loi de 1901-Journal Officiel.
(12) La Maconnerie sous l'occupation- de Andre Combes-2001-
(13) The Grand Lodge of France today- www.gldf.org
(14) La Declaration des Principes- www.fm-fr.org

THE SAINT DOMINGUE- LOUISIANA CONNECTION
by Ray W. Burgess, P.G.M. (Louisiana)

On Christmas Day 1492, Christopher Columbus, in the course of his voyage in search of a route to Asia, landed on an island in the Caribbean Sea, which he named La Isla Espanola, later known as Hispaniola, becoming the first Spanish colony in this part of the world. He later founded the City of Santo Domingo. The western part of the island was to become the French colony Saint Domingue and the larger eastern part the Dominican Republic.

The only inhabitants on the island were friendly Taino (Arawah) Indians adorned with golden ornaments. Sensing that they would gain "profitable things without number," Columbus ordered that a town and fortress be founded and that it be named La Navidad.

Leaving about thirty men behind, Columbus sailed back to Spain to bring colonists and supplies to recover gold and to develop the island. Returning in 1493 with about one thousand colonists, he discovered that all those left behind from his first voyage were dead. Undeterred, he set about building another fort and town that he called La Isabela. His main purpose was to find gold, which the Tainos said existed in the Cibao area. Despite the arrival of many settlers, a large number who were gold prospectors, the development of the colony was neglected. About one thousand died from overexertion or disease in the gold mines and from fighting Indians.

The prestige of Hispaniola declined even more when gold and silver were discovered in Mexico and Peru. Many of the colonists left to seek their riches elsewhere, and the population of the island declined sharply. Agriculture was neglected, and Spain became preoccupied with larger and richer colonies elsewhere. Accordingly, the population of this island colony in 1545 amounted to no more than 1100 persons.

This allowed French and English pirates to establish a base on the island of Tortuga, situated just off the North coast. In 1641 they founded Port Margot on the western end of Hispaniola and before long controlled the surrounding area. After driving out the English, they occupied themselves with hunting wild cattle and swine, and farming. Despite efforts of the Spanish to dislodge them, the French spread along the north coast and even engaged in illegal trade with the Spanish inhabitants. Finally, in 1697, under the Treaty of Ryswick, Spain formally ceded Saint Domingue to France. To build up the new possession, agriculture was encouraged and young women from France were brought in to marry the men.

In the seventeenth century, the principal crops were tobacco, cocoa, and indigo grown by small proprietors, aided by indentured servants and a few slaves. By the end of the seventeenth century, the population of this French Colony included about 6000 adult white and mulatto males and approximately 20,000 black slaves. Then came sugar cane, cotton, and coffee, all of which were labor intensive crops. Any terrain that would not permit cultivation was given to pasture. Consequently, the importation of slaves became a necessity for the large plantations. It has been estimated the population of Saint Domingue in 1789, on the eve of the Revolution, consisted of 35,500 whites, 26,000 free black (mulattoes), and 450,000 slaves. Thus, the whites were enjoying unparalleled prosperity.

During the eighteenth century Saint Domingue was the wealthiest colony on the globe. Its pomp and nobility rivaled that of the courts of Europe. The planters lived in luxury, and many spent much of their time in Paris. It was said the colony had attained a degree of brilliance that threw every other colony in the shade. The soil poured forth immense wealth that united its commerce with Europe and America. Fifteen hundred ships took on this rich production and freighted it to France. However, all of this was attained by the exploitation of close to a half million black slaves. A spark could ignite a confrontation that would make the French revolution in the mother country pale by comparison,

The spark was struck in early 1791 when a young Mulatto, Vincent Oge, demonstrated against the governor and was put to death. Before long, the colony was torn by riots. Slaves deserted their masters, burned and pillaged, and massacred every white man, woman and child on whom they could lay their hands.

One of the leaders of the rebellion was Pierre DominiqueToussaint L'Ouverture, an ex-slave who possessed considerable knowledge of military tactics and had natural leadership and political acumen. His loyalty would switch from the French to the Spanish to the French then finally to his own political ambition, all for the purpose of creating the Republic of Haiti. Even though he died in a French prison in 1803, his goal had been fulfilled, when, on January 1, 1804, the independence of Haiti was proclaimed.

From the start of the insurrection in August 1791 until the colony was finally abandoned in November 1803, white refugees fled to safety. Some went to France; a large number escaped to Cuba and Jamaica; others took flight to Atlantic ports from Georgia to Massachusetts; and some found their way to Louisiana. Most of those who immigrated to Louisiana originally settled in Cuba, where they began to recoup their fortunes by establishing coffee and sugar plantations. However, when Napoleon invaded Spain in 1808, the Spanish authorities expelled the French, and most of them fled to New Orleans in the summer of 1809.

This brings us to that part of the story which involves the lives and deeds of four refugees: Pierre François DuBourg, Louis Casimir Elizabeth Moreau Lislet, Yves LeMonnier, and Jean François Canonge.

Whereas this section is dedicated to Pierre François DuBourg his family was located, it would not be complete without including information about his brother, Louis Guillaume Valentine. In the Bibliotheque Nationale in. Paris can be found among the genealogical records, a "Maintenance de Noblesse," dating back to 1623, which was deposited there by a young nobleman of France by the name of Pierre DuBourg, as he was about to start on an extended trip, "on the point of undertaking a long journey." Thus the Louisiana branch of this patrician family begins with. "M. Pierre DuBourg, ecuyer et Capitaine de Navire."

Circa 1765, DuBourg and his wife Margurite, the former Margurite Vogluzan, migrated to Saint Dominque, where he became the owner of the immense plantation estate of Rochemont.

On February 16, 1766 a son, christened Louis Guillaume Valentine, was born. When he reached the age of two years, he was sent to France to be educated for the Catholic Church. He finished his seminary studies, and became head of a Sulpician school at Issy, near Paris. Because of in the French Revolution he was forced to leave and by disguising himself was able to reach Paris, where he made his way to the superior branch of the Sulpician. The revolutionists had also invaded that place, capturing the head of the institution and executing him. Rev. DuBourg, hiding at a friend's home, escaped with his life when the terrible September massacres took place. Disguising himself again, he fled Paris, reaching Bordeaux where his family was located. He found his life doubly in danger for the revolutionists were slaughtering churchmen as well as aristocrats. Knowing that he would not be safe in any part of France, he went to Spain and a little later sailed for America, reaching Baltimore, Maryland in 1794.

So capable did Rev. DuBourg prove to be, that within two years he became President of Georgetown College. Under his able management it became one of the leading universities in the United States. President George Washington honored it with a visit while still under the management of DuBourg.

The Abbé DeBourg also founded St. Mary's College and prevailed on the Legislature of Maryland to raise it to the rank of University.

Rev. DuBourg left Baltimore about 1800 for New Orleans, Louisiana where he began service at St. Louis Cathedral. In 1812 he became the first Archbishop of the Diocese of New Orleans. In this capacity he welcomed General Andrew Jackson at the door of the Cathedral and conducted him into the edifice to attend the Mass in honor of the victory at the Battle of New Orleans.

In 1818 he founded "An Academy for Young Gentlemen" which was later to become St. Louis College.Archbishop DuBourg died on December 12, 1833 in Montauban, France.

Another son, Pierre François DuBourg, who became known as Sieur de Ste. Colome, was born on December 30, 1767. He too was educated in France and later in England. Upon returning to Saint Domingue, he became involved in the management of Rochemont Plantation and eventually succeeded his father as owner. During the slave revolt in 1793, he escaped to Jamaica and in 1797 married Demoiselle Elizabeth Charest de Lauzon, daughter of M. François Charest DeLauzon and Demoiselle Perrine Therese de Gournay. The marriage contract shows all as residents of "Quartier de la Marmelade, Island of Ste. Domingue, now by reason of the misfortunes of the colony, refugees in the town of Kingston, Jamaica." Pierre François DuBourg and his family then came to the United States, and remained for a short stay in New Orleans before continuing on to Baltimore, taking with them their little daughter, Agláe. She was left to be educated at the Order of Sisters of St. Joseph, popularly known as the Sisters of Charity, which Abbé DuBourg had assisted in founding.

Leaving Baltimore, the DuBourgs returned to New Orleans and made their home with his wife's parents, who lived on Dumaine Street. New Orleans was a bustling business place at that time and offered great opportunities. DuBourg became a merchant and succeeded beyond his greatest hopes, repairing his heavy financial losses, and once again occupying a prominent position in both the social and business world. After three years' residence in the United States, he became an American citizen. He was a Major in the Louisiana Volunteers, held the position of Collector of the Port of the City of New Orleans, and was Counsul of the Kingdom of Sardinia. He was a broker, representing Michel Doradou Bringier and a number of other wealthy Louisiana planters. He served as Finance Minister for Governor Claiborne and as Major General on the Governor's staff.

DuBurg owned a large plantation called "Plaisance," which was located near where the street is today; and situated as most of them were at that date, a short distance back from the River Road. Louisiana Avenue is located in the center of what was then his plantation.

DuBourg became a Mason in 1805 and was a member of the LaParfaite Union (Perfect Union) Lodge No.29. He was elected Worshipful Master and played a very important leadership role in the New Orleans Masonic community.

By Act of Congress on April 8, 1812, Louisiana was admitted into the Union as a sovereign state. The territorial form of government had always been distasteful to the French population; therefore, Louisiana becoming a state was hailed with joy. This change in the political status of Louisiana had a corresponding influence upon Masonry, and measures were taken for the formation of a Grand Lodge. Perfect Union Lodge No.29, headed by W∴ Pierre François DuBourg, initiated the movement by inviting the seven lodges in New Orleans to send delegates to a meeting called for April 18, 1812. After presenting their credentials, the delegates organized themselves into a "General Masonic Committee of the State of Louisiana to provide for the establishment of a Grand Lodge in the City of New Orleans." Pierre François was elected President and even though two of the lodges withdrew, he successfully guided the group to its ultimate goal of forming a Grand Lodge, which occurred on June 20, 1812 DuBourg was elected as our first Grand Master and was reelected in 1813 and 1814.

M∴W∴ DuBourg died on January 29,1830 and was buried in St. Louis Cemetery No.2. He and his wife had five daughters, all of whom married into very prominent families in New Orleans.

It is very interesting to note that while Pierre was Grand Master, his brother was Archbishop of the Diocese of New Orleans. Even more ironic is that when Perfect Union Lodge built its original hall, it was forced to locate in Faubourg St. Mary, because the Roman Catholic Church authorities would not allow the structure to be built within the city limits.

The tale of the 'Brothers' DuBourg is unique. Two brothers were born into a rich aristocratic family with ties to the nobility of France. Both were educated in the best schools in Europe. One was steered toward service to the Catholic Church. The other followed a business career. One fled for his life because of the French Revolution and the other because of the slave insurrection in Saint Domingue. These similar events led them to America, where each distinguished himself; one in the field of education and religion, the other in business and Masonry. Their lives converged in New Orleans, where one attained the highest office in the Catholic Church in Louisiana, and the other the highest office in Masonry. The DuBourg name will long he remembered in the history books of Louisiana.

Louis Casimir Elisabeth Moreau Lislet

Louis Casimir Elisabeth Moreau was born in Dondon, St. Martin Parish, Saint Domingue on October 29,1767. His father, Jacob Vincent Moreau was a militia officer, Captain of the Limonade Battalion. His mother was Elisabeth Torel Moreau. She was compelled to spend much time in France for treatment of a disease that could not be cured elsewhere. She died tragically in 1793 when the schooner "The Delaware" was wrecked during a voyage from Le Cap Français, Saint Domingue to Philadelphia, Pennsylvania.

Not much is known of his early years other than to assume he lived the life of a wealthy son of a large land-owner. He attended a secondary school in Cap Français and studied law in Paris where he received the title of " Avocat au Parlement." In 1789, while in Paris, he married Ann Elisabeth Philippine de Peters. In 1790 they returned to Saint Domingue and settled in Cap Français, where he became "Premier Substitute de Procureur General au Conseil Supereeur de Saint Domingue, a position equivalent to that of first assistant public prosecutor or assistant district attorney.

The surname "Lislet" was given to him to distinguish him from his brother, Beniamin Moreau. Even after his brother was deceased, he kept the surname.

Soon after his return to Saint Domingue, the slaves, under the leadership of Toussaint L' Overture, rebelled and forced the whites to flee their country. Most of them, including Bro. Lislet, sought refuge in Cuba. In 1799, Napoleon dispatched a large army to the island and defeated the blacks, forcing them to flee to the hills. Bro. Lislet and many of his countrymen returned, but in 1803, the French troops were so decimated by yellow fever they were easily defeated by the blacks, again forcing the whites to flee.

Many of these refugees eventually arrived in New Orleans, without any possessions, but with an indomitable will to rebuild their lives and to resume their Masonic labors. Bro. Lislet and a number of other officers and brethren were members of the Lodge "la Réunion Désire" No.3013, which had been chartered by the Grand Orient of France at Port Au Prince, April 16, 1783. During the revolution, its charter, archives, etc. were destroyed. On February 15, 1806, they held a meeting and a lodge was opened by the old officers, Bro. Lislet serving as W.M. They resolved to resume their labors in New Orleans until such time as they could return to their old homes and to ask the Grand Orient of France for a duplicate charter. In a "provisional election" of officers, Bro. Lislet was elected W.M. The records close with the minutes of November 27, 1808, which was probably the last meeting of the lodge. No doubt this was due to low attendance and because an assessment of four dollars per month had been imposed upon the members (Does this sound familiar?). The records are in the possession of Perseverance Lodge No.4. The purchase of Louisiana in 1803 by the United States, brought an influx of Masons from other states, resulting in the chartering of lodges by the Grand Lodges of Pennsylvania and New York. Bro. Lislet was specially deputized to constitute these lodges and to also install their officers.

On June 13, 1812, a meeting was called by Bro. P.F. DuBourg, W.M. of Perfect Union Lodge No. 29 for the purpose of organizing a Grand Lodge of Masons for Louisiana. At its organizational meeting, Bro. DuBourg was elected Grand Master. 1818, he was elected Grand Master, and Bro. Lislet was elected Deputy Grand Master. In 1818, he was elected Grand Maser, after having served as Deputy Grand Master for six consecutive terms. He served with distinction and wisdom, guiding the Grand Lodge through some perilous times involving interference from other factions and jurisdictions.

Early in 1804, Congress divided the Province of Louisiana into the Orleans Territory and the Louisiana Territory. Bro. William C.C. Claiborne was appointed governor of the Orleans Territory.

The qualities and talents that Moreau Lislet displayed earned him the respect he justly deserved. Accordingly in June 1806, the Legislative Council and the House of Representatives of the Territory of Orleans named him and James Brown, "to draft and organize an adequate Civil Code for this Territory." In March of 1807, Governor C.C. Claiborne, appointed him Judge of the Parish of Orleans, which position he held until April 1813. He served on a Commission to plan a new college for the University of New Orleans and on the Board of Directors of the New Orleans Library. He held the position as the attorney for the City of New Orleans.

In 1815 he was elected to the Senate of the State of Louisiana, but resigned in early 1817 to become Attorney General of the State. He occupied this post until 1818 when he was elected to the House of Representatives, where he served until 1826, when he was again elected to the Senate. This was the last office to which he was elected and marked the end of his political career.

His professional ability, his intellectual gifts as an attorney and his virtues and qualities of character brought him many rewards. However, his personal life was wrapped in tragedy. His mother and son perished in a shipwreck. The death of his wife in 1809 left his daughter Elisabeth as his only close relative and when she was murdered, he retired into his home on Conde Street (now 1027-1029 Charters Street) where he died on December 3, 1832. He was interred in St. Louis Cemetery No.1 in New Orleans. His tomb is located on St. Louis Alley facing Conti Street.

Yves Julian Joseph LeMonnier

M:W: Yves Julien Joseph LeMonnier, the son of Rene LeMonnier and Ann Marie Viel, was born February 28, 1772 at Rennes in Bretagne, France. The LeMonniers were a family of physicians and scientists, dating back to the seventeenth century. Among them we find botanists, painters, philosophers, astronomers, and especially physicians and surgeons. An ancestor was the physician to Louis XIV.

Your researcher has discovered very little about his boyhood other than he attended the best schools and lived the life of opulence among the aristocracy. He attended the College Royal du Rennes and probably earned his medical training at that institution.

Shortly after reaching the age of manhood (1791) he and his older brother, Rene, migrated to Saint Dominque (Haiti) probably because of the French revolution. They acquired a coffee plantation and other property in Cap-Français (Parish). He also engaged in the practice of medicine among the French residents of the region.

Most of the coffee plantations were tended by slaves introduced from Africa, which in 1790 numbered 450,000 or more. The slave uprising, under the leadership of Pierre Dominique Toussaint L'Ouverture, was cataclysmic in its affront to production from the more than 800 plantations that were in the hands of the grands blancs-the rich.

Many of the French colonists including Yves LeMonnier were driven from their homes and settled in Cuba. Their settlements were chiefly in the vicinity of Santiago, de Cuba, where they introduced the culture of the coffee-plant, and being men of intelligence and education, flourishing plantations soon replaced the native forests. But their misfortunes were not yet over, and they were not destined to reap the fruits of their patient industry. In 1808, Napoleon invaded Spain and placed his brother Joseph on the throne. This aroused the national prejudices of the Spanish officials in Cuba against the French refugees, whose rich possessions whetted their rapacity. An order expelling all French subjects, and confiscating their property, was accordingly issued.

It was carried into execution with heartless rigor, and the unfortunate colonists resolved to seek asylum in the United States. The proximity of Louisiana to Cuba, and the fact that it had been originally settled by the French, induced the refugees to select New Orleans as their new home. Thus in May 1809, Yves LeMonnier chartered the Brig Fair America, commanded by Captain Abraham Barges, to transport his party, their baggage and slaves from Santiago de Cuba to New Orleans, arriving at Balise (a port at the mouth of the Mississippi River) June 21, 1809.

Since many of the early settlers of New Orleans were French, LeMonnier had no trouble fitting into the life of the city. He lost no time in resuming the practice of medicine and became one of the best known and respected doctors of New Orleans.

Charles Gayarre, in an address before the New Orleans Medical and Surgical Association, on December 3, 1887, described Dr. Yves LeMonnier as "a pale complexioned, modest, mild-mannered man, with a soft, low voice, and eminently prudent in his mode of treatment. His system seemed to be to leave nature to her free action and powers of recuperation, whilst merely assisting her in her efforts to cure herself." He had a trick of violently rubbing his nose when a case assumed a grave aspect, so that it was a matter of importance for a patient's friends to notice whether the doctor's proboscis had itched during the visit.

Dr. LeMonnier served with distinction during the Battle of New Orleans, prompting a certificate to be issued by President Andrew Jackson on October 13, 1829, which reads:

"I do hereby make known to all whom it may concern that Dr. Yves LeMonier, during the campaign of 1812-15 in the army under my command as chief surgeon of the uniformed battalion of the city militia, which corps was engaged in all operations that terminating in the retreat of the invading army and that Dr. 182 LerMonnier's conduct was such as to meet my warmest approbation."

He also donated his services to relieve the distress of many victims of the yellow fever epidemic which prevailed in New Orleans.

In 1811, Yves LeMonnier and François Grandchamps purchased the lot and unfinished building located on the southeast corner of Royal and St. Peter Streets for the sum of $16,000. They immediately engaged the services of two well known engineers and architects: Arséne Lacarriere Latour, General Jackson's principal engineer during the Battle of New Orleans, and Hyacinthe Laclotte, the engineer whose spirited engraving of the famous battle has been frequently reproduced. They set to work and on November 13, 1811 the "first sky-scraper" building (three stories) was completed and ready for occupancy, and the $7,600 promised the architects for their work was paid.

Doctor LeMonnier moved into the two upper stories and selected for his study the beautiful corner oval room on the third floor. The ground floor was rented for shops. From its corner window one can look at the iron-girded balcony which still bears his exquisitely wrought "YLM" mono- gram.

In 1814 he married Marie Charlotte Aimée Bouchet St. Martin, daughter of Pierre Bouchet St. Martin and the late Genevive Decalogue St. Martin of the Parish of St. Charles at the German Coast (Des Allemands). From this union were born four children: Amire, René, Ann Celeste, and Aimée.

Soon after arriving in New Orleans, LeMonnier became a member of Charity Lodge No. 93. He was Junior Warden of the Lodge in 1812 when he was selected to serve on the "special committee for the formation of the Grand Lodge." He was subsequently elected Grand Pursuivant.

In 1816-1818 he served as Grand Junior Warden; in 1819 Grand Senior Warden; and in 1820 was elected Grand Master.

Sometime in 1821 Charity Lodge No. 2 (formally No. 93) became extinct. Its records break off abruptly July 8, 1821, and there is no documentary evidence as to the cause of its dissolution. Yves LeMonnier, a Past Master of the Lodge, and Past Grand Master in 1820, became Worshipful Master of "Loge les Amis Reunis, No.7787 (Friends of Order). Since this was a French Rite Lodge and since Charity Lodge had no French Rite members, it is more than probable that the question of Rites being mooted in the lodge is the reason for its dissolution.

Early in March, 1829, an arrangement was completed by which Les Amis Reunis Lodge No.7787 became attached to Perseverance Lodge No.4, and the members of each Lodge became active members of the other other. The Lodge was annexed to Perseverance Lodge in 1833.

M∴W: LeMonnier was one of the group of petitioners who appeared before the Senate and House of Representatives, State of Louisiana, in 1816 for the purpose of incorporating the Grand Lodge. He also served on the committee that directed the ceremonies in connection with the visit of the Marquis de Lafayette to the Grand Lodge in 1825.

M∴W: Yves Julien Joseph LeMonnier died on June 6, 1832 and was interred in St. Louis Cemetery No.1, New Orleans Louisiana. His burial site cannot be located.

Jean François Canonge

The paternal side of the Canonge family was originally from Marseilles in Provence, France. The parental head of the family to bear the name Canonge was the Marquis de Jussan, a French Nobleman of high standing, who served with merit in the armies of Louis XV. According to a commission dated 1747, signed by the Monarch and countersigned by Marc Pierre de Voyer, Comte d'Angenson, Minister of War, the Marquis was appointed to a lieutenancy in a company of huzzars.

At a later time the Marguis de Jussan, becoming enthusiastic over the wonderful things he heard about Saint Domingue, emigrated to this West Indian paradise. He married an heiress to a large fortune and of one of the finest domains at Jeremie. Mme. de Jussan was gifted with a nature of highest distinction which shone with a brightness seldom seen even in the fashion halls of Paris.

The Jussan family owned many slaves but kind treatment by the owners was equally proverbial. When the slave uprising swept over the country in a savage wave, their servants hid the members of the family in the woods, brought them food, and by their watching attention protected them from the bands who were slaughtering and burning.

When the emigration of 1804 occurred, many of their slaves followed them to Cuba and subsequently to the United States. One of these faithful slaves, Antoine by name, came with the family to New Orleans.

The Marquis de Jussan had one daughter, Renée de Jussan. She married Jean Benjamin Canonge, a very rich resident of the island, where he exercised great influence because of his intelligence, extreme liberality and benevolence, and a possession of a large fortune. He died before the flight of the family to Cuba. From the marriage of Jean Benjamin and Renée de Jussan, were born; Auguste Canonge, Jean François Canonge (the subject of this paper), Benjamin Canonge, Z.B. Canonge, Aurore Canonge, and Elizabeth Aimée Canonge.

Jean François Canonge was born in Jérémie, Saint Domingue, in 1785. He was reared in Marseilles, France, under the guardianship of his uncle, Major F. Canonge, chevalier of St. Louis, an officer of distinction in the French Army. Major Canonge was a second father to his nephew, who, when recalled by his family, left Marseilles with much regret.

After leaving Cuba, the family repaired to Philadelphia, PA. In a short time J.F. Canonge became a naturalized citizen and studied law under a celebrated attorney named Duponceau, a Frenchman by birth, who served with Washington during the War of Independence. After being admitted to the bar, he decided on New Orleans as the place of his future residence because the French element was largely represented in the posterity of the early settlers of the Louisiana Colony. At the time of his arrival, the French and English languages were both used on the floors of the State Senate and the House of Representatives and, as a consequence, the clerks of these bodies were required to report the French speeches in English and the English speeches in French. He filled the position of Clerk of the House of Representative for several sessions. Possessed of an incomparable memory, he took no notes of the discussions and debates, although it often occurred that translations had to be made from one language into another, without omitting any important feature.

Standing foremost in the ranks of lawyers of that day, he was for some time associated in the practice of law with the celebrated and profound American lawyer, John R. Grymes. He made his capacities felt as an orator, linguist and impromptu speaker on special occasions. His success at the bar secured for him, from Gov. A.B. Roman, the appointment of Judge of the Criminal Court of New Orleans, at that time a court unique in its character because there was no appeal from its decisions. In this position, which he held for ten or twelve years, he distinguished himself by the manner in which he conducted himself. In his days of incumbency of judgeship of the Criminal Court, the Louisiana Supreme Court was presided over by Judge François Xavier Martin. On a certain occasion Judge Martin intimated to Judge Canonge that he should grant a new hearing on a capital case that had been brought before the latter. Judge Canonge refused so the Supreme Court ordered his imprisonment for contempt of Court. This caused Judge Canonge to order the arrest of the five Judges of the Supreme Court. The matter was finally settled when the Supreme Court finally acknowledged the legality of the position taken by Judge Canonge.

The first mention of Bro. Canonge's Masonic activities occurred in 1818 in Philadelphia, PA, when he served as the Grand Senior Warden of the Cerneau Grand Council of Princes of the Royal Secret, 32°. Also, in 1818, he became an Honorary member of Perseverance Lodge, leading one to conclude that he resigned his membership in the Cerneau Body and moved to New Orleans.

In 1820 he was Grand Senior Warden of the Grand Lodge of the State of Louisiana; in 1821, he was Deputy Grand Master; and he served as Grand Master in 1822,1824,1826-27, and 1829. He was Worshipful Master of Charity Lodge No. 2 in 1821, and of Etoile Polaire Lodge No.5 in 1824. He was a member of Les Amis Réunis Lodge No. 7787 and Perseverance Lodge No.4 in 1829. This was brought about when an arrangement was completed by which Les Réunis Lodge became attached to Perseverance Lodge, and the members of each lodge became active members of the other. Each lodge had its own officers with the exception of the Treasurer, who filled that office for both Lodges.

On April 25, 1836 he affiliated with the Grand Consistory of Louisiana. He was created a 33°, Inspector General Honorary on March 8, 1838 by J .J . Conte and served as Lt. Grand Commander until March 22, 1843, when he was elected Grand Commander in Chief of the Grand Consistory of Louisiana, which office he held until April 1, 1846. Bro. Canonge was elected Sovereign Grand Commander of the Supreme Council of the United States of America, sitting in New Orleans on September 20, 1845 and held that office until his death. It is likely that Bro. Canonge gave up the office of Commander in Chief of the Grand Consistory due to his election as Grand Commander of the Supreme Council. The same year that he gave up the position of its Commander in Chief, the Grand Consistory passed under the jurisdiction of the Supreme Council, and after his death the Supreme Council was changed to The Supreme Council of Louisiana.

On November 8, 1847 he participated in the ceremonies to lay the corner-stone for the State Capitol building in Baton Rouge. He delivered an oration that was very critical of the intrusion of the Grand Lodge of Mississippi into Louisiana. This was probably the last note-worthy Masonic act in which he participated before his death.

Bro. Canonge married the young widow, Mme. Amelung, née Amellié Mercier, daughter of Jean Mercier and Maria Garcia de Fontenelle. She was a perfect type of Creole, who shone in the world of Paris with the same brilliancy that she dazzled the social set of New Orleans. Gifted with a fine intelligence, she possessed artistic tastes, and handled the brush with talent. She died in Paris November 10, 1830, aged thirty-eight years.

From this marriage were born Alphonse, Hippolyte, Laure, J. Placide, Emma, and Ernest. All of their children with the exception of Laure, who died in infancy, were educated at the College Louis-le-Grand, Paris. Ernest, who became a member of the Louisiana House of Representatives, completed his studies at Jefferson College, St. James Parish.

Alphonse Canonge was, like his father, a prominent lawyer in New Orleans. He, also, served with distinction in the capacity of Superintendent of public schools. Another son, J. Placide Canonge, was an eminent journalist, author, and actor.

M∴W∴: Jean François Canonge died January 19, 1848. He is interred in St. Louis Cemetery No.2, New Orleans. Louisiana.

References

Perusse, Roland I. "Historical Dictionary of Haiti." The Scarecrow Press, Inc., Metuchen, N.J., 1977.

Weil, Thomas E.; Clack, Jan Knippets; Blautstein, Howard I.; Johnston, Kathryn T.; McMorris, David S.; Munson, Frederick P., (Coauthors) "Haiti, A Country Study." The American University, Foreign Area Studies, Washington, D.C., 1973

Bell, Ian "The Dominican Republic" Westview Press, Boulder, CO, 1981.

Stoddard, T. Lothrop "The French Revolution in Santo Domingo." Houghton Mifflin Company, Boston, MA, 1914.

Brasseaux, Carl A. and Conrad, Glenn R. (edited and annotated) "The Road to Louisiana." The Saint- Domingue Refugees 1792-1809. The Center for Louisiana Studies, University of Southwestern Louisiana University, Lafayette, LA, 1992,

Dawson III, Joseph G. (edited by) "The Louisiana Governors." Louisiana State University Press, Baton Rouge, 1990.

Scot, James B., "Outline of the Rise and Progress of Freemasonry in Louisiana, " New Orleans, 1923.

Levasseur, Alain A. "Louis Casimir Elisabeth Moreau Lislet," Louisiana State University, Law Center Publications Institute, Baton Rouge, 1996,

Holleman, Elizabeth Sullivan and Cobb, Isabel Hillery "The Saint Domingue Epic." The Nightingale Press, Bay St. Louis, MS, 1984.

Escalle, E. and Guillaume, M. Gauyon, "Franc- Macons Des Loges Francaise ' Aux Amerques' , 1770-1850. Paris. 1993.

WHAT IS TRUTH?
by Michael R. Poll, P.M.
Secretary, Louisiana Lodge of Research

A few weeks ago I tuned in to one of the educational channels on TV and watched a show on archeology. It was an interesting show dealing with the history of archeological practices from the early "Indiana Jones" style to today's standard of documentation. I found a general similarity between the growth and development of archeological excavation standards and those of Masonic research. The show pointed out that in the early days of archeology, researchers would find an important site and boldly their way in to take whatever they felt was valuable or important with little regard for detailed documentation or preservation of the site. Today, great care is taken at excavation sites. It is realized that value and importance are not only with items, but where they are located, what might be near them and the general condition of everything having to do with the site. In the old days of Masonic research, importance was given to special events, but less care was made in verifying the events or knowing what was going on at the time of the event. It is realized today that the whole story, and the understanding of the whole story, entails far more than isolated events.

Technology being developed today is also of great importance to both archeology and Masonic research. Ground penetrating radar allows archeologists to "see" below ground. When these devices are rolled over an area with buried ruins of past civilizations, the whole area becomes visible and they know where they should begin their dig. In addition, satellites are being employed to help with archeological excavation in overgrown forest areas such as South America. The satellites are able to filter the forest and discover sites which previously would have been discovered only by luck.

Likewise, Masonic research has been greatly aided by advances in technology. Where at one time a Masonic researcher would need to travel hundreds or thousands of miles to sit in a Masonic library to wade through large stacks of paper documents, today the computer and internet can put all of the world's great libraries at his fingertips. Databases of information and documents can allow a Masonic researcher to locate, read and copy documents physically located most anywhere in the world from the researcher's home computer.

While technology allows researchers to locate items of value far more quickly than in past times, the need to understand an item of interest and what it means remains vital. Finding an old Masonic diploma means little more than momentary interest if you know nothing of the individual or body for which the diploma was issued.

And this brings us to Louisiana.

There are few places with a richer research potential than Louisiana. Simply put, Louisiana is a Masonic researcher's gold mine. When we couple the large amount of unanswered questions in our Masonic history with modern technology, the potential for great discoveries is enough to excite any thinking researcher. We have an opportunity in Louisiana that is greater than many realize.

But, there is another side to every coin. In this case, the other side of the coin is lack of understanding. It is one thing to find or possess an important Masonic document. It is another thing to properly understand it. The danger exists for important old documents to be found, appreciated only as "something old" and then hidden away in private collections unavailable and lost to all.

Louisiana is, by any way you look at it, unique. Our government, laws and Masonry are, to this day, different than in other parts of the United States. Louisiana was founded as a French territory. It was French in nature, language and custom. French Masonry was introduced into Louisiana some sixty years prior to the creation of the Grand Lodge of Louisiana.[1] The five lodges who created the Grand Lodge of Louisiana were French-speaking lodges.[2] This was not done because of any particular loyalty to France or any desire to *not* be a part of the U.S., but simply because this is what the vast majority of the Louisiana Masons knew. They spoke French, not English, and they practiced their Masonry in the manner in which they knew it.

And what of the English-speaking Americans who began arriving in New Orleans soon after it became a U.S. territory in 1803? Most of the rank and file Americans traveling to the city did not speak French. Yet, the government, shops and pretty much everywhere you went was French-speaking. Sure, the educated on both sides were multi-lingual and able to function in either society, but the majority of the population were not the educated leaders. The same was true in Masonry. English-speaking Masons arriving in New Orleans on business trips wanted to visit lodges. But, the language being used in New Orleans lodges was mostly (save one or two) not to their understanding and even the furnishings and practices that could be understood were not the same American-Webb ritual familiar to them. What visiting Masons saw in New Orleans was mostly very different from what they knew. And, at that time, "different" was not a good thing.

Unrest was born in both the population of the city of New Orleans and in Louisiana Masonry. On one hand, the English-speaking Masons of New Orleans demanded that change take place and Masonry in Louisiana be turned into the Masonry of the rest of the country. On the other hand, the French-speaking Masons saw no need to bring about such change when their Masonry had been the same for as long as they knew it. It was the establishment in Louisiana. It was the Masonry as worked in Europe and the Masonry with which they were comfortable. Both sides were unyielding and unwilling to work with the other side.

In 1851, John Gedge was elected Grand Master of the Grand Lodge of Louisiana. His election places him in a status held by no other Grand Master of our Grand Lodge. You see, prior to his election as Grand Master, MWBro. Gedge was viewed by the Grand Lodge of Louisiana as being an *irregular* Master Mason. Not only was he viewed to be an irregular Mason, he was the *Grand Master* of a Grand Lodge viewed to be irregular. But, it does not end there. Gedge was Grand Master of this Grand Lodge in 1848, 49 and 50. Without missing a beat, he stepped from being Grand Master of a Grand Lodge viewed as irregular to Grand Master of the Grand Lodge of Louisiana. Why? How? Of course, we are talking about the *Louisiana Grand Lodge of Ancient York Masons* and its 1850 merger with the Grand Lodge of Louisiana, but why did the Grand Master of the "irregular side" step right over to become the Grand Master of our Grand Lodge? This event can be seen as one of the catalysts to the great unrest, division and bitterness in New Orleans Masonry in the mid 1800's, but who was right and who was wrong? Do we have enough information to form any sound conclusion?

During the trial of Jesus, the Roman governor Pontius Pilate asked what would seem to be a straightforward question: "What is truth?" Since that time, philosophers have pondered and debated both the question and its answer – many times with less than satisfactory conclusions.

In the 1970's, a movie was released that has risen today to the status of a classic - *Star Wars*. Designed to be a science fiction/ adventure film, the move had a few surprising philosophical elements - possibly from one of the script advisors, Joseph Campbell. With a careful eye, Masons might find some things of value in the events presented in the tale.

The story is about a young boy, Luke Skywalker, who lived on a farm in a far away galaxy. Luke was raised by his aunt and uncle after the death of his parents. He worked and lived simply, but was aware of a war taking place in far-away parts of his galaxy. That was the truth that he knew.

One day, while he was away, the war came to Luke's planet. His home was attacked and his aunt and uncle killed. An old man, who was viewed by Luke as something of a hermit, took him in. His name was Obi-Wan Kenobi. Luke began to learn amazing things from and about this old man. He learned that Obi-Wan had been a warrior in the very war that was being fought – a Jedi Knight who was highly skilled and possessed great powers. But, Luke learned more. He learned that the powers of a Jedi are passed down from parent to child. Luke learned that he possessed these same powers because his father was also a Jedi Knight who fought in the very same war. Luke knew nothing of this and his reality began to change. What he knew as "the truth" was not actually the truth. Luke asked about the actual fate of his father. Reluctantly, Obi-Wan told him that his father was killed. He told him that a gifted student of his turned to the "dark side" and killed his father. The student's name was Darth Vader.

Luke continued to train and grow in power. Then one day he left to face the man who killed his father. Luke and Vader faced each other in Jedi battle. When Vader realized who Luke was and that he was trained by his former master, he asked Luke if Obi-Wan told him of his father. In anger, Luke told him that he was told enough, that he knew that Vader killed his father. In the bombshell of the movie, Darth Vader then tells Luke, "No, Luke, *I* am your father." Luke was devastated. He screamed in anguish and broke away from the fight. It was not only clear that he, once again, did not know the actual facts about his father, but now he must face that his own *father* was the ultimate villain causing so much trouble in the galaxy. Luke's concept of truth seemed to be proven faulty time and again. What *was* the truth?

When Luke again saw Obi-Wan, he wanted to know why he had been told falsehoods. Surprisingly, Obi-Wan told him that what he told Luke *was* the truth, "from a certain point of view." He explained that his father, Anakin Skywalker, was a good man and when he fell to the "dark side" the good man was killed by the evil that became Darth Vader. Obi-Wan then said, "Luke, you're going to find that many of the truths we cling to depend greatly upon our own point of view."

I needed to think long and hard about that line by Obi-Wan. Maybe sometimes truth is subjective.

In matters of religion, truth does seem to fall very much in line with the thoughts of Obi-Wan. My truth may or may not be your truth. It depends upon our own point of view. How many wars have been fought in the name of religious truth? How many men have been willing to die, or kill, in the name of religion? How do you prove a religious truth? The poet Kahlil Gibran wrote, "Faith is a knowledge within the heart, beyond the reach of proof." Religious truth is accepted as such simply because we believe it.

In its wisdom, Masonry realized early on that good, honest men could have very different religious views. As such, pointed religious (or political) discussions are not allowed in lodge. The outcome of such discussions could result in disharmony. It is the combination of the passion in which a religious or political view is held along with the inability to conclusively prove such views that result in such discussions being emotional powder kegs. One simply does not prove the correctness of a religious view or political opinion in the same manner that they would prove a mathematical equation.

Religion and politics are not the only subjects which can result in passion for a Mason. Masons have a passion for Masonry. Masons very often have a *strong* passion for Masonry. Want to see a good fight? Get two Grand Lecturers together who disagree as to if it should be "on" or "upon." We are taught to subdue our passions, but, truthfully, do we always?

So, let's go back to the mid 1800's and keep these thoughts of "passion" and "truth" in our minds.

In New Orleans, the city that care forgot, there were two groups facing off. They differed in language, Masonic customs, Masonic rites, and points of view. They were emotional. They were passionate. They were unyielding. It was not a case of two friends sitting down with one ordering strawberry ice cream and the other chocolate and enjoying each others company. It was a case of two angry opponents sitting down disgusted that the other would dare to order something different than their flavor. The *truth* held by each was that their flavor was the best! Period. They were childish. Each group of Masons held to their own "flavor" of Masonry and would tolerate no difference of opinion as to the validity of their view. It was not a case of "you are mistaken;" it was a case of "you are a liar." It was a sad, sad time.

The two sides in New Orleans refused to bend or try to understand the other. Rather than withdrawing to avoid disharmony, they openly engaged each other in lodge or in public settings with bitter and unMasonic attacks upon the character of their brothers.[3] It was a war. It was a nasty war. It was not necessary.

From a strictly historical standpoint, we know some of what took place, and some of the "why." But, there is much that remains unknown or unclear about the events prior to the "wars." We know but bits and pieces of pre-1850 Louisiana Freemasonry.

We have lessons and opportunities.

The lessons should be obvious. We are taught to subdue our passions. We are taught to not speak evil of our brothers – either to their face or by private character assassination. We should try to help each other, not wage war on each other because we have differences of opinion as to the nature of Freemasonry. We should advance the Light of Masonry, not the darkness of ignorance, falsehood and ambition.

Our opportunities should also be obvious. Never before has technology been available to make the work of Masonic research easier and more possible for anyone with the desire. We have clear standards of how our research should be conducted, documented and presented. We know that we should not present ideas as facts, or allow "Masonic politics" to color or sway our research or presentation. We have the chance to do meaningful, objective work that can benefit the Freemasonry of today as well as the future.

The brothers of the mid 1800's were quick to point the finger of blame at "the other guy" for all the perceived wrongs in Masonry during that time. But, were the wrongs with Masonry itself or the individual Masons of the time? Was Masonry flawed on either side or were the individual Masons flawed? Can we see the opportunity to help Masons of today by a study of the unfortunate events of the past?

When our ego allows us to see clearly, we realize that Masonry is better than us. Masonry is not improved because of our membership; we are improved because of our membership.

We have an opportunity. We have the tools to do the real work of Masonic research. We have the knowledge to know the nature of the real work of Masonic research. It is up to us to either do that work and earn our keep as Masons or succumb to the three villains.

What is truth? It may depend on what we are made of and our own points of view.

Notes:

1. On Sunday, July 16th, 1752, Loge de la Parfaite Harmonie was created in New Orleans under the direct jurisdiction of Loge de la Parfaite Union de Martinique. Sharp Document #40.
2. Parfaite Union #1, Charité #2, Concorde #3, Persévérance #4 & Etoile Polaire #5.
3. Among other works, see: A Masonic Trial in New Orleans by Joseph Lamarre, tans. by Charles Laffon de Ladébat (1858); Mémoire à Consulter by James Foulhouze (1858) and A Dissection of the Manifesto of Mr. Charles Bienvenu by Albert Pike and Charles Laffon de Ladébat (1858).

WHITHER ARE WE TRAVELING?
by Dwight L. Smith, P.G.M. (Indiana)

Chapter 1
Whither Are We Traveling?

The Wailing Wall is crowded these days. Masonic leaders, great and small, are lined up, each awaiting his turn to lift his voice in lamentation. The figures show a falling off of membership. Attendance at Lodge meetings is not what it used to be. The thing to do is to adopt this project or that gimmick, and then all will be well. As might be expected, the projects and gimmicks are about as impossible as they are ridiculous.

For several years, the bosom-beating has been going on. Firing with a shotgun rather than a rifle, our leadership has offered little of a constructive nature. Prescriptions for the most part have consisted merely of sales talk for whatever pet scheme was being proposed. Only a few voices in the wilderness have made a mature and realistic appraisal.

I. Faulty Diagnosis

At the outset, I may as well precipitate an argument by disposing of the old favorites:

One: Whatever attendance troubles our Lodges may be having are not caused by television, nor the automobile, nor by bowling, nor togetherness, nor any of the other "busyness" in which our restless society is engaged. A multitude of activities may contribute to a decline in Lodge attendance, but they do not constitute the cause. When we complain of lack of attendance, what we really are saying is that *interest* is at a low ebb, for in any organization, if there is interest, there will be attendance. No amount of television or bowling or endless "busyness" can usurp the position of eminence a Lodge of Freemasons occupies in a man's loyalty if the Lodge is in a position to command his loyalty.

The ailment isn't quite that simple. We are looking at the symptoms – not the disease. The real source of the trouble is within ourselves.

Two: Such problems as we may have will not be solved by forcing men to memorize a set of questions and answers, nor by cramming books and lectures down their throats, nor by any Big Brother Plan, nor by devoting our energies and resources to other organizations or movements, however worthy they may be.

47

The cure isn't that simple, either. The patient's indisposition will not be relieved by nostrums. The treatment, too, must come from within.

II. Basic Premises

Next, may I offer what I consider to be three basic premises. Then we shall get down to cases.

First: The history of Freemasonry is one of ups and downs. If this brief period is one of the "downs," it is nothing compared to some of the crises through which our Fraternity has passed.

Second: In our membership decline, we again see history repeating itself. It simply is a case of our sins catching up with us. We had a decade in which there was a membership influx that was both unhealthy and unhappy. We ran a production line; we counted new members by the hundreds of thousands; but we could count new Masons only by the score. Now comes the payoff.

Third: Whatever is wrong with Lodge attendance in 1962 was wrong 25 years ago when I was Master of my Lodge. I doubt seriously whether Lodge attendance ever has been "what it used to be." I had to work by head off to sustain interest in 1937. Sometimes I succeeded; sometimes I didn't. The situation is no different today; tomorrow and the day after it will be the same.

I repeat: we have only to look at ourselves to discover the cause for whatever unhappy days have come upon us. Our troubles are of our own making. Such corrective measures as we take must go beyond the surface; they must go to the roots of the problem or be of no avail.

Then let's take an honest look at some of the conditions within our own house which may be contributing to a membership decline and a tapering off of interest.

III. Self-Examination

1. **Let's face it! Can we expect Freemasonry to retain its past glory and prestige unless the level of leadership is raised above its present position?** On many an occasion in the past 14 years, Masters and Secretaries have come into my office to ask my advice on what to do about lagging interest. Again and again I have said, "There is nothing wrong with your Lodge, nor with Freemasonry, that good leadership will not cure." I believe that.

2.**How well are we guarding the West Gate?** Again, let's face it. We are permitting too many to pass who can pay the fee and little else. On every hand I hear the same whispered complaint, "We used to be getting petitions for the degrees from the good, substantial leaders in the community. Now we are getting. . . ." Just what it is they are getting, you know as well as I.

3.**Has Freemasonry become too easy to obtain?** Fees for the degrees are ridiculously low; annual dues are far too low. Everything is geared to speed— getting through as fast as possible and on to something else. The Lodge demands little and gets little. It expects loyalty, but does almost nothing to put a claim on a man's loyalty. When we ourselves place a cheap value on Masonic membership, how can we expect petitioners and new members to prize it?

4. **Are we not worshipping at the altar of bigness?** Look it in the face: too few Lodges, with those Lodges we do have much too large. Instead of devoting our thoughts and energies to ways whereby a new Master Mason may find a sphere of activity within his Lodge, we let him get lost in the shuffle. Then we nag and harangue at him because he does not come to meetings to wander around with nothing to do. We are hard at work to make each Lodge so large that it becomes an impersonal aggregation of strangers – a closed corporation.

5. **What can we expect when we have permitted Freemasonry to become subdivided into a score of organizations?** Look at it. Each organization dependent upon the parent body for its existence, yet each jockeying for a position of supremacy, and each claiming to be the Pinnacle to which any Master Mason may aspire. We have spread ourselves thin, and Ancient Craft Masonry is the loser. Downgraded, the Symbolic Lodge is used only as a springboard. A shortsighted Craft we have been to create in our Fraternity a condition wherein the tail can, and may wag the dog.

6. **Has the American passion for bigness and efficiency dulled the spirit of Masonic charity?** The "Box of Fraternal Assistance" which once occupied the central position in every Lodge room has been replaced by an annual per capita tax. That benevolence which for ages was one of the sweetest by-products of the teaching of our gentle Craft has, I fear, ceased to be a gift from the heart and has become the writing of a check. And unless the personal element is there, clarity becomes as sounding brass and tinkling cymbal.

7. **Do we pay enough attention to the Festive Board?** Should any reader have to ask what the Festive Board is, that in itself will serve to

show how far we have strayed from the traditional path of Freemasonry. Certainly the Festive Board is not the wolfing of ham sandwiches, pie and coffee at the conclusion of a degree. It is the Hour of Refreshment in all its beauty and dignity; an occasion for inspiration and fellowship; a time when the noble old traditions of the Craft are preserved.

8. **What has become of that "course of moral instruction, veiled in allegory and illustrated by symbols," that Freemasonry is supposed to be?** If it is a course of instruction, then there should be teachers, and if ours is a progressive science, then the teaching of a Master Mason should not end when he is raised. I am not talking about dry, professorial lectures or sermons – heavens no! That is the kind of thing that makes Masonic education an anathema. Where are the parables and allegories? Alas, they have descended into booklets and stunts. No wonder interest is so hard to sustain.

9. **Hasn't the so-called Century of the Common Man contributed to making our Fraternity a little too common?** We can not expect to retain the prestige the Craft has enjoyed in the past if we continue without challenge to permit the

standards of the picnic ground, the bowling alley, the private club and the golf links to be brought into the Lodge hall. Whether we like it or not, a general lowering of standards has left its mark on every Lodge in Indiana, large and small.

10. **Are there not too many well-meaning Brethren who are working overtime to make Freemasonry something other than Freemasonry?** It was an unhappy day when some eager beaver conceived the idea that our Craft should adopt the methods of the service club, or the luncheon group, or the civic league, or the Playboy outfit. Whoever the eager beaver was, he lost sight of the fact that one of the reasons our Fraternity is prized so highly is that it does *not* operate like other organizations.

Well, that should be enough for one dose. The following pages elaborate on the ten points enumerated above. Let me give you fair warning. In the following essays I shall call a spade a spade. Some of my readers are not going to like it. But what I have to say I believe our Craft needs to hear, and it is only for the "good of the Order" that it is said.

I shall propose no bright new ideas – not one. All I am going to advocate is that Freemasonry remain Freemasonry; and if we have strayed from the traditional path, we had better be moving back to the main line while there is yet time to restore the prestige and respect, the interest and loyalty and devotion that once was ours.

Chapter 2
The Level of Leadership

Question 1: Can we expect Freemasonry to retain its past glory and prestige unless the level of leadership is raised above its present position?

A teacher in the public schools of a neighboring State cherished a long-standing desire to become a Master Mason. His petition to the Lodge in which he resided was accepted. He presented himself for the Entered Apprentice degree, but never returned. The Brethren of the Lodge concluded, I am sure, that they had made a mistake in electing that Entered Apprentice because of his apparent lack of interest.

But it was not lack of interest that caused him to go out of the door, never to return. It was disappointment and disillusionment. The performance of the Master of that Lodge was such that it constituted an insult to the candidate's intelligence. Because the head of the Masonic Fraternity in that community was careless and sloppy and crude, because he was attempting to do something for which he was not prepared, because he was trying to give "good and wholesome instruction" on subjects he knew nothing about, a good man was lost to Freemasonry.

On first hearing, that story made a profound impression upon me. The more I have thought about it, and the more I have seen it duplicated, the more I am convinced that the Number One responsibility for any tapering off of membership, any lack of interest and attendance, rests squarely upon the shoulders of our Lodge leadership.

Yes, I know the subject is a touchy one. But in introducing it, I am only putting into print what has been whispered in the corridors these last ten years.

Take a long and thoughtful look at the names of the men who served our Lodges as Master 100 years ago – or even 50 years ago. Consider the positions of importance those men occupied in their respective communities. Then let us ask ourselves whether our present day leadership is in the same league.

One unforgettable Lodge meeting stands out in my mind. The Lodge was having trouble maintaining interest; membership was dropping; it had called for help. When the hour came for the meeting to begin, there had been no preparation. I sat around waiting for Lodge to be opened; sat around waiting for dinner to be served; sat around while the candidates were being prepared; sat around while the Junior Warden tried to enlist a craft, actually calling for volunteers, wheedling, cajoling;

sat around while the Master, reluctant to close, literally begged those on the sidelines to say a few words. In short, *I sat around.* What was there in that meeting that would make anyone want to come again?

Nor do I exempt myself. Looking back on some of the meetings the year I was Master, it is a wonder to me the Lodge held together. Many of my meetings were such a first class bore that I would do almost anything to avoid getting trapped in such gatherings today.

If we want our Lodges to regain the position they once occupied in the interest and loyalties of men, we had better gain a proper perspective; we had better sort things out in the order of their importance. To open the discussion, permit me to make three pertinent observations:

1. **We must pay more attention to proficiency in the East.** We make a great to-do over proficiency of candidates. We want to devise some method whereby new Master Masons may be forced to memorize a set of questions and answers. But we do little or nothing to insure proficiency where it really counts.

A Master is expected to be Master of his Lodge – not a weakling to be pushed around. Theoretically, he "sets the Craft to work and gives them good and wholesome instruction." Yet what do we require for election as Master? Simply that a Brother serve as a Warden. That is all. There are no minimum requirements as to ritualistic proficiency; nothing regarding history, symbolism, philosophy, ethics, law, tradition. Only a so-called degree for Past Masters which, in far too many instances, is a farce. We elect a Master and expect him somehow to become a leader. It never occurs to us to require evidence of leadership first.

2. **There is far more to being Master of a Lodge than the mere recitation of a ritual.** We are paying the penalty of years of "mass production" practices, and a bitter penalty it is. When Masters of Lodges are so lacking in imagination and vision that they cannot conceive of a Masonic meeting unless a degree is conferred, then we need not expect a revival of interest and attendance and we need not look for an upswing of membership short of war.

I would a thousand times rather see as Master of a Lodge a man who can provide real leadership, a man who can give "good and wholesome instruction," a man who comprehends what Freemasonry is all about, even if he cannot confer a single degree. Suppose he can not recite the ritual. So what? There always are those who are eager and willing to do ritualistic work, but there are precious few who can provide inspired leadership.

It is high time we start looking about for the best possible leadership and enlisting the support of men who can lead. But instead, we consider only those who come to Lodge, those who stick it out in the endurance contest. We "start in line" the man who is on hand whenever the door is opened regardless of whether he has even the most elementary qualities of leadership.

If the practice of automatic ladder promotion of officers must be discarded in order to obtain the kind of leadership we should have, then by all means let us discard the foolish custom. There is nothing in the winning of an endurance contest, in itself, that qualifies a man to be Master of his Lodge.

If the so-called "line" of officers must be shortened to enable men of ability to serve their Lodges without devoting six or seven years to minor offices, then what are we waiting for? Why not shorten the line? Is not good leadership for one year more important than keeping a seat warm for six?

3. **If Freemasonry is to command respect in the community, then the man who wears the Master's hat must be one who can command respect.** The young teacher who did not return for advancement because his entire conception of Freemasonry was colored by what he saw and heard in the East. The Master of a Lodge is the symbol of Freemasonry in his community. If he is not a man upon whom intelligent people may look with admiration, then we need not expect to reap a harvest of petitions from intelligent men.

Make no mistake. Men judge Freemasonry by what they see wearing Masonic emblems. They judge a Lodge by the caliber of its leadership. If we persist, year after year, in putting our worst foot forward, then we can expect to continue getting just what we are getting now.

Chapter 3
Asleep at the West Gate

Question 2: How well are we guarding the West Gate?

Down in Tennessee many years ago I heard one of the old stalwarts express the conviction that unless a Lodge is rejecting at least 20 per cent of its petitioners, it is either very fortunate or very careless. That striking statement has come to my mind many times in recent years. Unquestionably the good Brother had a point.

But 20 per cent, mind you, is one petitioner out of every five. (In Indiana we are rejecting about one petitioner in every twelve). It is not difficult to visualize what would happen if an Indiana Lodge were to reject one petitioner in five. The Grand Lodge office would be besieged with delegations; the Grand Master would be implored to do something to stop the "epidemic" of black-balling.

Of course, the rejection of one petitioner in five might, in the long run, be the best thing that could possibly happen to a Lodge, but we are not interested in taking the long term view. No, we want to get the new Temple paid for.

For years now I have heard the whispered complaint, "We used to be getting petitions for the degrees from the good, substantial leaders in the community. Now we are getting.Isn't it about time we stop our whispering and say some things out loud, even if they are unpleasant to hear?

One of the conditions causing dismay in more than one Lodge is the fact that the sons of its highly respected members are not petitioning for the degrees. True, they may be busy getting ahead in the world; they may not have the money; they may not be interested. But that is not all.

Why should intelligent young leaders in the community petition a Lodge if they have little or nothing in common with its members? If they cannot find in Freemasonry a social, intellectual and cultural atmosphere that is comfortable, they will find it elsewhere.We like to repeat the story about Theodore Roosevelt, as President of the United States, attending Lodge when the gardener on his estate was Master. (We don't say how often he went.) But I daresay if the membership of that Lodge had been predominantly gardeners, even the extrovert T.R. might have been a little lax in his attendance!We can not escape the fact that men judge Freemasonry by what they see walking down the street wearing Masonic emblems. And if what they see does not command their respect, then we need not expect them to seek our fellowship.

Let's face it. Thanks to two wars, inflation, the cost of building and maintaining expensive Temples, and a general lowering of standards, thousands of men have become

Masons who should never have passed the ballot. The inevitable result, then, is that the Craft is not looked upon with the same degree of respect it once enjoyed.

How did it all come about?

1. **Economic pressure, for one thing.** A Lodge pays a heavy price for a new Temple so costly to maintain that membership must remain above a certain figure.

2. **We have fallen into careless ways in the investigation of petitioners.** There was the regrettable incident in my own Lodge one time when I served on an investigating committee. The petitioner was widely known; apparently he was worthy; at least nothing to the contrary had reached my ears. Accordingly I turned in a favorable report. The petitioner was elected. Several months later, from another source, the bombshell burst. Not until then did I learn that it was common knowledge about town that the petitioner was far from worthy. To correct the mistake there had to be some embarrassment and some unpleasantness. It has been a sobering thought to reflect that many of my Brethren may have questioned the petitioner's worthiness, but gave him the benefit of the doubt simply because I had made a favorable report!

Whence came the idea that a man – almost any man – has an inherent right to become a Freemason? Is it not a privilege to be conferred upon the worthy?

And whose idea was it that if a petitioner was rejected, a grave injustice has been done the petitioner? Is no one interested in seeing that an injury is not done the Lodge and all Freemasonry by electing one whose worthiness may be in question?

Such an Open Door Policy is not selectivity; it is come-one-come-all. And Freemasonry is a selective organization. It must be if it is to avoid the fate of a score of fraternal groups whose names are well nigh forgotten.

3. **Lodges are not utilizing their most capable members for duty on investigating committees.** In every Lodge there are Brethren of high standards who love the Fraternity and want to see its good name protected; men who would make more than a token investigation; men would really stand guard at the West Gate.

But are such men appointed as members of investigating committees? Not unless they happen to be present at a stated meeting when a petition is received. You have heard it innumerable times: "On this p'tition, I'll 'point Brother Joe Doak, Brother Jim Jones and Brother Bill Brown." Just like that, the deed is done—the most important assignment ever made in a Lodge is made with no more thought than would be given to who shall turn out the lights. In the hands of Joe Doak, Jim Jones and Bill Brown rests the good name of Freemasonry, even though they may know nothing at all about making an investigation, and care less. But Joe Doak, Jim Jones and Bill Brown were present at a stated meeting – perish the thought that one *not* present be used now and then!

All of us have seen Masters appoint investigating committees literally hundreds of times, but on how many occasions have we seen evidence of careful thought in the selection of personnel for those committees? Men of high caliber and ability are available. Why are we not using them? Is it for fear they might turn in an unfavorable report?

You have heard me say it before and you shall hear me say it as long as I have a voice and a pen: in Freemasonry, there simply is no substitute for quality. We are accepting too many petitioners who can pay the fee and little else; too many men who have no conception of what Freemasonry is or what it seeks to do, and who care not one whit about increasing their moral stature; too many men who look upon Ancient Craft Masonry with contempt – who are interested in using it only as a springboard from which to gain a prestige symbol.

And we had better start applying the brakes while there is yet time.

Chapter 4
Pearl of Great Price?

Question 3: Has Freemasonry become too easy to obtain?

Some three months ago when this series of articles was introduced, I took advantage of a fifty-year presentation occasion to write a Masonic editorial. The recipient of the Award of Gold had petitioned a Southern Indiana Lodge in 1911 when he was making $10 a week as an apprentice printer. The fee for the degrees was $20. He thought enough of Freemasonry to empty his pay envelope twice.

A century ago it was not uncommon for men to pay what amounted to a month's wages to become a Mason. We know without challenge that today petitioners are paying a fee which represents a week's wages at the most – sometimes only two or three days!

When we compare the nominal dues paid to a Lodge of Freemasons with those paid to a service club, a labor union, a trade or professional organization or a country club, we begin to get a faint idea of the source of some of our troubles.

And when we compare the ridiculously low fees paid to an Ancient Craft Lodge with the aggregate fees paid to other Masonic bodies and appendant groups, we begin to see clearly what is wrong. Men are willing to pay for the privilege of Freemasonry, but we distribute the fee they should be paying to an Ancient Craft Lodge among all the relatives, the in-laws and the step-children. We place such a cheap value on the basic degrees that it is no wonder newly raised Masons end up having little or no respect for the Symbolic Lodge.

Before we are in a position to tackle some of the difficulties that beset us, we must reestablish the premise that Freemasonry is a Pearl of Great Price, worth a great deal of effort, a great deal of sacrifice, a great deal of waiting to obtain. We need to do a little preaching, perhaps, with a certain New Testament passage as the text: "For where your treasure is, there will your heart be also."

Has Freemasonry become too easy to obtain? I am one who believes that it has. And I am not the only one. My old friend Arthur H. Strickland, of Kansas, recently wrote a thoughtful article for The Philalethes, entitles, "Who Killed Cock Robin?" Calling attention to the old axiom that what is easy to get is not much appreciated, he observes that "we have done everything that we can think of to cheapen Masonry. . . .We have cheapened the Fraternity to the point that it is seriously reacting against us."

Has Freemasonry become too easy to obtain? To me, the question is not even debatable. For example:

1. Our fees for the degrees are so low as to constitute an insult to the Fraternity. When I petitioned for the degrees in 1933 the fee was $20. That was a good-sized chunk of anybody's money in 1933, but I would have paid three times that amount. Our economic standards of today can hardly be compared to 1933, yet the minimum fee in Indiana is still only $30—and one Lodge in five charges the absolute minimum. There is not a Lodge in Indiana whose fee should not be at least twice its present amount.

For a long time I have had the uneasy suspicion that the period of accent on quantity rather than quality may have started during those cut-rate years of 1933 to 1944 when the minimum fee was only $20.

2. Everything is geared to speed, as if a deadline had to be met. Freemasonry is no longer worth waiting for, nor working for, nor sacrificing for. Too often it is only a badge of respectability, a prestige symbol, to be obtained with the same hurry-up zeal that would be assumed in acquiring a Cadillac or a yacht. Candidate A must be rushed through the degrees before he leaves for service in the armed forces (he has heard it might be helpful to him.) Candidate B must be rushed through because he is about to move to a distant point to take a new job. Candidate C must hurry through so he can join a class in some other organization.

Proficiency? Nonsense! A friendly coach can take care of that. Comprehension of the underlying philosophy of Freemasonry, its symbolism and ethics and traditions, what it is and what it seeks to do? You know the answer to that question as well as I.

And we not only permit such a situation – we actually encourage it. How, in Heaven's name, can we so cheapen Ancient Craft Freemasonry and expect anything other than contempt for the parent body?

3. **The privilege of courtesy work has been so abused that it actually has become a detriment to all Freemasonry.** What was once intended as an occasional pleasant arrangement for the benefit of a Lodge has been liberalized to the point that it now is only for the convenience of a candidate. Do you realize that a candidate for the three degrees may become a Master Mason without ever having attended a single meeting of the Lodge which has elected him? He can be initiated in one Jurisdiction, passed in another, raised in another. And yet we expect him to become a loyal and devoted Mason, with a strong sentimental attachment to a Lodge he knows nothing about, and which has done nothing except to elect him! We crave his faithful attendance, but we do about everything in our power to create a situation in which loyalty has no place.

The incident in Montana in which a Brother received his fifty-year button without ever having attended a meeting of his own Lodge is not as far-fetched as we would like to think.

We can learn a great deal from our Mother Grand Lodge of England and from the Jurisdictions of Scotland and Ireland, Australia and Canada, where a candidate must receive the Entered Apprentice degree in the Lodge that elected him, and in no other. It was a sad day for Masonry in Indiana when that regulation was repealed.

4. **One of the worst offenders in the cheapening process is the well-meaning father who is too eager for his son to become a Mason.** Those are hard words, but I have seen the story repeated over and over again. Sonny must be pushed through because Pop wants him to join the class in another body; because Pop wants him to receive the degrees in Germany, or France, or South America. Sonny may not have even lived within the Jurisdiction of the Lodge for years and years, but Pop wants him to join if the Lodge has to violate all the rules in the book to accomplish it.

So Pop comes to the Grand Lodge office with a plea that the residence laws be set aside; that the period of investigation be waived; that Sonny be advanced without regard to proficiency. You have known him; so have I. His name is legion.

What a contrast to the spirit of that great and good Past Master of an Indianapolis Lodge who waited years upon years to hear his son express the desire to become a Mason—and who, even then, did not offer to pay the son's initiation fee because he wanted the boy to appreciate what he was getting!

And then there are the ill-advised church parishioners who pay the fee for their minister. I have met quite a number of those ministers in my day, and have become rather cynical after working long hours trying to unravel their record of suspensions for NPD. But I must not get started on that subject.

When we downgrade Ancient Craft Masonry, submit it to all sorts of indignities, look upon it with contempt, label it as something hardly worth mentioning, permit it to have only the crumbs that fall from the table, what can we expect if Master Masons no longer give to their Lodges their full measure of loyalty and devotion?

Chapter 5
The Closed Corporation

Question 4: Are we not worshipping at the altar of bigness?

One of the most serious trend in American Freemasonry is the development of the oversized, impersonal Lodge. Even though such a condition is utterly foreign to all the traditions of Freemasonry, little or nothing is being done to correct it. On the contrary, Lodges are encouraged and expected to become even larger. What the result will be, no one knows. It may require a crisis of the first order to bring us to our senses.

The entire philosophy of Freemasonry is built around the individual – the erection of a moral edifice within the heart of a man. All its symbolism is individual symbolism; all its tradition and practice is aimed at making individuals wiser, better, and consequently happier. Mass movements simply have no place in Freemasonry, and never have had.

Then why do we worship at the altar of bigness? For one thing, we are Americans. We measure civilization in terms of automobiles, TV sets and bathtubs. We count the number of gadgets as shown in the census reports and assume that means we are more civilized.

In the United States, the average membership of Masonic Lodges is about 252; in Canada's nine Jurisdictions, 166; in the seven of Australasia,

117; in Puerto Rico, 92; in Scotland, 85; in England, 80; in Mexico, 70; in Germany, 53.

Interestingly enough, the small Lodges overseas have little or no attendance problem. The Brethren receive a *summons* to attend their Lodge and they attend because it is worth attending, and because the membership is small enough that there is a congenial, closely knit unit— a community of interest, if you please. And certainly no one can accuse the overseas Lodges of not "doing things." In their benevolent work and in their impact on community life, they put us to shame.

In the 49 Jurisdictions of the United States average membership ranges from a high of 482 in the District of Columbia to a low of 115 in North Dakota. There is even a Lodge in Kansas with some 5,700 members. (I almost hesitate to mention the fact for fear some of our itchy Hoosier Brethren will set out to exceed that record of doubtful distinction.)

Only nine Jurisdictions have a higher average membership per Lodge than Indiana's 336. They are all in densely populated States. (It will give us grave concern, I am sure, to know we are tenth instead of at the top.)

Is all this talk some curious notion the Grand Secretary has all by himself? Not at all. Some of the best minds in American Freemasonry are deeply concerned. Speaking of poor Lodge attendance, Past Grand Master Ralph J. Pollard, of Maine, observes: "This problem is probably inherent in our American system of large Lodges and relatively low dues. It is one of the prices we pay for bigness and cheapness … Probably the best long-range cure will be found in more and smaller Lodges where more Brethren can be put to work and where a warmer and more intimate fraternal spirit can develop."

And in a masterly address before the Conference of Grand Secretaries in North America in February, 1962, Dr. Thomas S. Roy, Past Grand Master of Massachusetts, observed, "If we permit our Lodges to increase in membership to a size inconsistent with a close fellowship, then we have created the conditions for non-attendance. The Grand Lodge of England is chartering new Lodges in England at the rate of over twenty-five a year. It is of some significance that, according to the latest figures, the average membership in all Lodges under the Grand Lodge of England is roughly eighty."

II

What happens when we worship at the altar of bigness?

1. **Well, in the first place, our annual waste of leadership is nothing**

short of a sin. Every year our Lodges welcome into Masonic membership hundreds of men with a great potential for inspired, dedicated leadership – and then we make certain they will have no opportunity to exercise it. Only one Master can serve in a given Lodge per year. We close the door on the best we have because we are too shortsighted, too solicitous of numbers and bank account to divide our membership into smaller units and utilize the manpower that is going to waste.

2. **We provide too few opportunities for new members to use their talents, and then wonder why they lose interest and drift away.** I have heard Lodge officers complain bitterly about new members coming once, twice, three times, and then no more. But why should they come when there is nothing for them to do except listen to the minutes and allow the bills? There is no place for them; worst of all, no one seems to care.

3. **The fellowship of Freemasonry does not thrive in the mass.** When will we ever learn that fellowship, that sweet and precious jewel of our Brotherhood, is an intimate thing not shared with great numbers? Some of the most priceless memories of my 28 years as a Mason center around individual contacts with just a few of my Brethren in the Lodge room and about the table – those times when we were doing things together, rejoicing in prosperity, standing steady in adversity – *but always together.* Thank God there weren't a thousand of us. If there had been, I daresay my interest in Freemasonry would have withered on the vine years ago.

What must be the feeling of a newly raised member when he discovers that his Lodge, which promised him fellowship and intimate friendships, is but a huge, impersonal aggregation of strangers – a Closed Corporation!

And we wonder why the membership curve goes downward, and why Masons do not attend meetings of their Lodges!

III

What are we doing about it? Just making certain that new Lodges will be formed, that's all. Then why aren't we at work on a long range, patient effort to correct a serious condition?

1. **Well, first of all, remember, we are Americans, and in all areas of life we worship at the altar of bigness.**

Two men came to my office to talk over what had to be done to form a Lodge in a rapidly growing community. Let us call the community Suburbia. One of the Brethren made a significant statement that has been ringing in my ears from that day to this: "In my Lodge of more than 1,500 members," he said, "I haven't a ghost of a chance to ever go through the chairs. A new Lodge at least would give me the chance." That Lodge was never organized, because a neighboring Lodge sent a committee to serve notice on the Brethren that *"We regard Suburbia as a stock pile for our Lodge."*

2. **Then, we are not at work organizing new Lodges because a new Lodge might cause some inconvenience to a horde of organizations now occupying quarters in our Temples.** Scores of Masonic Temples in Indiana have room for one or two additional Lodges, but house only one. Instead of encouraging Lodges of Ancient Craft Masonry, which should be occupying our Temples, we shut the door on them in favor of groups which have attached themselves to Freemasonry's coattails. Isn't that statesmanlike thinking?

I am not worried about Lodges that are too small and too weak. That condition will eventually take care of itself. What disturbs me is the number of Lodges that are too large – and that condition is *not* taking care of itself. What possible reason is there for boasting that Brotherly Love Lodge is the largest Lodge in the city or in the state? That should be cause for apology rather than rejoicing. Brotherly Love Lodge should be devoting its energies to the extension of its influence in other areas – but you can bet that Brotherly Love Lodge will do nothing of the sort. It might lose a few dozen members.

Truly, "the harvest is plenteous but the reapers are few." Scores of Indiana cities and towns could use another Lodge, or two or three, to the good of all Freemasonry. The population is here, and, in most instances, facilities could be made available. But first we must get over our foolish idea that in order to be effective a Lodge must be large, and wealthy, and own a lush Temple in which 5 per cent of its membership or less can huddle together on meeting nights.

What happens to an institution designed to be simple becomes complex, when units meant to be small become oversize and unwieldy, when work intended for many is restricted to a handful, when something that should be intimate becomes impersonal?

What happens? Look around. Exhibit A is all about us.

Chapter 6
Subdivided We Stand

Question 5: What can we expect when we have permitted Freemasonry to become subdivided into a score of organizations?

Back in my newspaper days I used to get a great deal of unwholesome amusement out of the power struggle between four church congregations in a town of less than four hundred inhabitants. All four churches were of the same denominational family and bore the same name. Each claimed to be the Real Thing. The membership of each was convinced that all others were heretics, and, as such, were condemned to eternal damnation.

What must a newly raised Master Mason who takes his Freemasonry seriously think of our subdivisions? Are they just as baffling to him as the four churches of the same name in a town of 400 were to me? Sometimes I wonder.

What must he think when he discovers that no less than 70 organizations have attached themselves to our ancient brotherhood – and that the end is not in sight? What is the reaction of the man who came into Freemasonry of his own free will and accord when he finds that a subdivision can solicit him almost as soon as he leaves the altar in the Entered Apprentice degree? And how does he feel when his beloved Lodge is referred to as the "Blue Lodge" with a rather patronizing air, and when the so-called "Blue Lodge Mason" is looked upon as something inferior, as if his neck and ears were not quite clean?

If we are interested in exploring possible causes for a decline in membership and for a slackening of interest and attendance, we had better look to our subdivisions. Of course, he who introduces the subject invites bitter criticism, but I stand firm on my conviction that in the United States we are spreading ourselves so thin that the basic unit – the Ancient Craft Lodge – is the loser. We may not end up by killing the goose that laid the golden egg, but certainly we are bleeding her white.

Yes, I am a member of many of the subdivisions. All of them have contributed much to my understanding and appreciation of Freemasonry, and I do not believe any of them can question my loyalty. *"It is not that I love Caesar less, but that I love Rome more."*

And I am not the only one who is concerned, — not by a great deal. Authorities by the dozen might be quoted. As long ago as 1924 the eminent English Masonic student, Sir Alfred Robins, was writing that "this sponge-like growth is spreading in American Masonry, and is threatening certain of the best interests of the Craft." One of the most forthright and statesmanlike pronouncements comes from Brother Noah J. Frey, 33°, Scottish Rite Deputy for Wisconsin, in an address before the Grand Lodge of Wisconsin in 1961. "Sometimes," he said, "I wish that Masonry were not as divisive as it is, because we are all Blue Lodge members, and I fear that we lose sight of that fact and divide ourselves into smaller groups and thereby increase our inefficiency."

And certainly Dr. Thomas S. Roy, Past Grand Master of Massachusetts, can not be accused of hostility to any Masonic body, yet in an eloquent address before the Conference of Grand Secretaries in North America in February, 1962, he was forced to declare:

"If we permit the proliferation of Masonry into rites, and the 57 varieties of bodies whose membership is dependant upon ours, let us face the fact that the attendance that goes to them belongs to us. There is a sense in which it can be said that their success is our failure. I am not passing judgment on any of them. I am a good member in some of them, and have done my share of work in them. But they all must face the fact that they must pour some of their strength back into the Symbolic Lodge. For any weakness we develop must sooner or later communicate itself to them."

It is not basic loyalty that is at stake; it is not unity of purpose that we lack. Nor can we gloss over our shortcomings with talk about money, and benevolences, and good works. *These are not the issues.* We have never faced the real issues, which are:

One: The weakening of the basic unit of Freemasonry by too great an emphasis on our subdivisions, and,

Two: The unsound premise that the child is more important than the parent. Let's stand before the mirror and take an honest look at ourselves.

1. **Masonic bodies and appendant organizations are actually competing for the time, the attendance, the interest, the substance, the devotion of Master Masons.** I am sick and tired of all the talk about TV, and the automobile, and bowling leagues as competing influences. It is time we look in our own house to see where the competition comes from.

Like the four churches of the same name, each Masonic organization poses as the Real Thing. Each claims to have That Which Was Lost. Each is the true wrinkle if we want to appear before the world as a Big Mason – one with a collection of degrees, exclusive and affluent.

2. **Our subdivisions have encouraged the mental attitude that when a Master Mason gains membership in another body, he then and there has outgrown the Ancient Craft Lodge.**

Several months after I became a Mason I was solicited by a worker in one of the recognized bodies. But I had mental reservations. "Why is it," I asked him, "that Masons who belong to the other bodies place such a stress on those affiliations and seem to care so little about their Lodge?" Just what answer he gave me I do not remember. Really, it doesn't matter too much, for the question never has been answered to my satisfaction. I held out for about three years before I presented my petition.

Years later, when I received the degrees in another Masonic body, I overheard a past presiding officer say, "Now here, in this body, you will find the Cream of Masonry." From that day to this, I have resented such artificial class distinction.

The newspaper obituary in my files which states that the deceased "was a member of 17 organizations, 10 of them Masonic groups," and then proceeds to list everything that could be bought with money, is a case in point. To be a Master Mason was not enough; actually, that was of little or no importance.

And what about the Vanishing Emblem? What is wrong with the Square and Compass? Even Grand Masters have discarded it. Is it no longer a badge of honor? Must something else replace it to set the wearer apart and place him in the aristocracy?

A young man of my acquaintance was interested in petitioning for the degrees. He was interested, that is, until a Master Mason gave him the old Superiority Sales Talk, something like this: "Sure, I'm a member of Brotherly Love Lodge, but only because I have to be. The Blue Lodge, it doesn't mean a thing to me. What I'm after is what give me the prestige and helps me in my business!"

And we wonder why attendance is poor, why interest is lax, why the membership curve goes downward!

3. **Then there are these subdivisions that foster the attitude that, within their place of refuge, the standards of Ancient Craft Masonry do not apply.**

Therein lies a situation that is more than alarming; it is downright vicious. Scarcely a Jurisdiction in the United States is free of headaches brought on by some group restricting its membership to Masons, but considering itself exempt from Masonic standards. A few Jurisdictions have met the issue head on, to the good of all Freemasonry. Others have looked in the other direction, and thereby have damaged the entire Fraternity.

One of these days Masonic leadership had better come to grips with the issue. The winking attitude which says, in effect, "It's none of our business as long as you are not wearing an apron," is unthinkingly dealing a body blow to our beloved Craft. A serious minded young friend of mine expressed interest in Masonry until a Past Master gave him a lurid description of the antics and the carousals he enjoyed in his favorite appendant organization. That ended his interest. Mark it down. *The public makes no distinction between the Master Mason who wears an apron and the Master Mason who wears some other kind of garb.*

4. **When the leadership of Ancient Craft Masonry neglects the parent body to smile upon everything which claims a relationship to Freemasonry, however remote, that leadership is not contributing to a solution of our problem; it is only aggravating it.** In a single year, not so long ago, two American Grand Masters actually visited more appendant bodies than Symbolic Lodges in their respective terms of office.

From one end of America to the other, Grand Masters are going up and down their jurisdictions like itinerate peddlers, promoting everything under the sun except plain, unadulterated Symbolic Freemasonry. They go to Washington to attend what used to be the Grand Masters' Conference and find that it has become "Masonic Week" with the side-shows taking over. Truly, the tail has begun to wag the dog. And we wonder what is wrong!

Subdivided we stand, and subdivided, I fear, we shall fall.

One does not have to be more than forty to remember when the superpatriots raged over the hyphenated American, declaring it was time to drop Old World loyalties and become an American without a hyphen.

Well, I am not advocating that hyphenated Masons eliminate anything that contributes to their understanding and appreciation of Freemasonry. But I am preaching a gospel of fundamentals. I am calling on our Symbolic Lodges to do a better job of upgrading themselves. And I am challenging the other Masonic organizations and appendant groups to put a stop to the down-grading of the Symbolic Lodge; to acknowledge by actions, rather than words, that the Lodge is the fountainhead of all Freemasonry; to put first things first; to look unto the rock whence they are hewn.

Chapter 7
Sounding Brass and Tinkling Cymbal?

Question 6: Has the American passion for bigness and efficiency dulled the spirit of Masonic charity?

Ask the average Hoosier Mason what has happened to Masonic charity and he will expostulate all over the place while rattling off an impressive list of organized, institutional projects of a benevolent nature. He will tell you that there is a Masonic Home at Franklin, hospitals for crippled children, research programs for mental illnesses, prevention of blindness, muscular dystrophy. If he is well informed he will tell you about a visitation program in Veterans' Hospitals.

Pin him down and ask him what his Lodge does in the way of benevolence. If he knows where and when his Lodge meets, he may tell you that a portion of each member's dues goes to help operate the Masonic Home; that sometimes a goodly sum is collected in voluntary contributions for the Home; . . . and besides, the dues of a hard-pressed Brother were remitted several years ago.

Press him still further and ask him what *he* is doing, as a Mason, to carry out his individual obligation. He will show you his collection of cards and enumerate the checks written to a dozen projects, and the income tax deductions claimed during the past year.

Then nail him to the mast and ask him, "Is that all? How long has it been since you went on foot and out of your way to aid and succor a needy Brother?" Chances are his look will be first one of astonishment; then of pity; then he will mark you down as well meaning, perhaps, but slightly off your rocker.

What *has* happened to Masonic charity? Time was when it was one of the sweetest byproducts of the teachings of our gentle Craft. I recall reading in the minutes of my Mother Lodge how the Brethren got together and built a modest house for the widow of a member, and on another occasion donated a cord of wood to the widow of a man who was not a Mason. Such acts were common. They were not accompanied by any fanfare of trumpets, but the community knew about them all the same, and the prestige of Freemasonry reflected that knowledge.

Only occasionally do we hear of an example of genuine Masonic charity at its best, but when we do, the impact upon the individual and community is tremendous. Why, then, do we neglect that phase of our Masonic life that can have the most gratifying results? What has happened? Two things, I should say:

One: We are Americans, you know, and we don't want our benevolence on an individual basis, quiet and modest, from one heart to another, even if that is the most effective manner. We want the right hand and everyone else to know what the left hand is doing. We want our charity to be well organized with campaigns, slogans, quotas and great hullabaloo. We want super-duper institutions with bronze plaques on the walls to say, like Little Jack Horner, "What a great boy am I!"

Two: When Freemasonry is operating properly, it does things the hard way. We want none of that. We want efficiency. We don't want to be bothered by anything that will require more time and effort than the writing of a check.

Now let no man throw up a smoke screen with a charge that the Grand Secretary is attacking organized Masonic charities. I am doing no such thing. What I am attacking is the laziness, the complacency, the lack of vision with which we pour great sums of money into organized benevolences, and then, with self-righteous congratulations to ourselves, let it go at that.

I

Wherein do we fall short? Let's look in the mirror:

1. **Is it worth mentioning?** — How often do we hear the Master call for reports of sickness at a meeting of the Lodge? In how many Masonic halls is the Box of Fraternal Assistance passed? In how many halls could such a box be found?

2. **Do we remember?** — How often are the members of a Lodge called upon to assist in person, in some act of true Masonic charity? Are they ever asked to visit the sick, or is that assignment turned over to a retired Brother who has nothing else to do? How many years can go by without a Master Mason giving of himself in an act of benevolence, or charity, or brotherhood?

3. **Are we interested?** — In far too many Lodges the payment of the annual per capita tax to the Grand Lodge is looked upon as the full discharge of all obligations pertaining to charity – an act which relieves every individual member of further concern for the year ending December 31. When I say that, unfortunately, I am not merely engaging in rhetoric; I am speaking of an actual fact.

4. **First things last?** — In far too many Lodges even the easy expedient of soliciting voluntary contributions for the Masonic Home is pushed aside as something of minor importance if there is a new Temple to build or pay for. Self-indulgence comes at the head of the list.

5. **Crumbs from the table?** — Each Lodge in Indiana is required to have a relief fund. But how much? I am ashamed to have the minimum figure seen in print. It is such a paltry sum that it could hardly do more than buy an occasional cup of coffee for a street beggar. The minimum should be twenty times its present amount.

II

But there is another side to the coin. Let's look at that side for a moment:

1. **Given the challenge to practice Masonic charity in its intimate**

and personal form, almost any Lodge and almost any individual Mason will respond with enthusiasm. More important, Freemasonry will then come to have a new meaning for them. A few years ago the Grand Master of Missouri, distressed by the perfunctory manner in which the charity obligation is discharged, set out on a campaign to encourage Lodges to perform their own acts of charity – voluntary acts, impulsive acts, without organization, without advance planning and ballyhoo. He asked each Lodge to send him a written report of what it had done. I read many of those reports, but not without a lump in my throat.

And not only in Missouri can it happen. Right here in Indiana I have seen glorious examples of Masonic charity. For example, the story of one small Lodge which came face to face with a staggering obligation, and of how the Brethren responded to their everlasting credit.

2. **Any Lodge, large or small, which experiences the joy of giving of itself in a truly personal act of charity discovers that it literally has been born again.** Once I heard the Senior Warden of a large Lodge describe the distress in the home of the widow of a deceased Brother who was making a brave struggle to hold her family together. "It is not often we have calls for relief," he said. "Now this is *our opportunity.*" Significantly, that Lodge is not losing in membership and has no attendance problems.

A Past Master of a small Lodge which levied an assessment to meet a relief emergency sat in my office and declared, "That incident was the best thing that has happened to our Lodge in the 40 years I have been a Mason, for, until then, most of us had no clear idea of the true meaning of Masonry."

III

What does it all add up to?

Well, for me, it adds up to this: We are missing a golden opportunity for a great Masonic renaissance when we continue to let our American passion for bigness and efficiency dull the spirit of true Masonic charity. There simply is no substitute for the personal touch on the local level where it counts.

Don't tell me how many hundreds of thousands of dollars Freemasons contribute annually to organized benevolent projects. That is not the question at stake. And don't give me the old excuse that Lodges are prohibited from using their funds for purposes not

Masonic. That, too, is avoiding the issue. Freemasonry, if it operates as such, is a relationship with individuals, and I insist on talking about the personal efforts of Lodges and individual Master Masons. I want to know what *individual* Masons are doing to relieve distress – in their own communities, by their own effort.

Whenever Lodge is opened and whenever it is closed, the Senior Warden tells the Master why he was induced to become a Master Mason. One of the reasons he offers is that he might "contribute to the relief of poor distressed Master Masons, their widows and orphans."

Lip service? Sounding brass and a tinkling cymbal?

Not unless we make it so. The Brethren are here; they are as generous and kindly and thoughtful as they ever were. It is up to us to give them occasion to do what they have obligated themselves to do. Given that opportunity, Master Masons will respond in such a manner that the revival of Freemasonry will no longer be a fond hope – it will be here and now.

Chapter 8
The Decline of Fellowship

Question 7: Do we pay enough attention to the Festive Board?

Pisgah Lodge at Corydon was less than a month old then the time came for celebrating the Fest of St. John the Baptist in 1817. There was every reason for dispensing with an observance – the Lodge was small, little or no money was to be had, and no doubt it was a busy time for the Brethren, for there were forests to be cleared.

But the minutes tell us that a tiny handful of Freemasons assembled and marched to the court house to hear an oration, "after which in proper order the members and visiting Brethren marched in procession to Mr. Boon's and partook a dinner prepared according to arrangement."

Yellowed records of any Lodge a century old and more will describe similar events at which the fine old tradition of the Masonic Feast was kept alive in spite of hardships on the Hoosier frontier. And if the faithful Secretary went on to record the amount spend for a jug of whisky with which to gladden the occasion, we chuckle indulgently and explain to ourselves rather weakly that times were different then.

Times certainly were different. And I am not at all convinced in the area of Masonic fellowship that the change has been for the better.

Back in February, when I first questioned whether we pay enough attention to the Festive Board, I went on to observe: "Should any reader have to ask what the Festive Board is, that in itself will serve to show how far we have strayed from the traditional path of Freemasonry."

Yes, of course, every Lodge has "eats" now and then – and too often that is just the word to describe it: eats. But how often are the Brethren permitted to meet around the Festive Board for the genuine, heart-warming fellowship of the traditional Masonic feast – the same kind of close-knit community of interest that a family experiences when it gathers for the Thanksgiving dinner?

By and large, Lodges have just about abandoned that happy camaraderie which for generations was extolled by Masonic orator and poet. H.L. Haywood, preeminent Masonic author and scholar of our age, writes in his book, *More About Masonry:*

In the Eighteenth Century Lodge the Feast bulked so large in the life of the Lodge that in many of them the members were seated at the table when the Lodges were opened and remained at it throughout the Communication, even when degrees were conferred. The result was that Masonic fellowship was good fellowship, as in a warm and fruitful soil, acquaintanceship, friendship, and affection could flourish – there was no grim and silent sitting on a bench, staring across at a wall. Out of this festal spirit flowered the love which Masons had for their Lodge. They brought gifts to it, and only by reading of old inventories can any present day Mason measure the extent of that love; there were gifts of chairs, tables, altars, pedestals, tapestries, silver, candlesticks, oil paintings, libraries, Bibles, mementos, curios, regalias and portraits. The Lodge was a home, warm, comfortable, luxurious, full of memories, and tokens, and affection, and even if a member died his presence was never wholly absent; to such a Lodge no member went grudgingly, nor had to be coaxed, nor was moved by that ghastly, cold thing called a sense of duty, but went as if drawn by a magnet, and counted the days until he could go.

What business has any Lodge to be nothing but a machine for grinding out the work? It was not called into existence in order to have the minutes read! Even a mystic tie will snap under the strain of cheerlessness, repetition, monotony, dullness. A Lodge needs a fire lighted in it, and the only way to have that warmth is to restore the Lodge Feast, because when it is restored good fellowship and brotherly love will follow, and where good fellowship is, members will fill up an empty room not only with themselves but also with their gifts.

Then let's proceed to the question I keep asking so persistently. What has happened?

1. **First of all, we must not underestimate the Puritan influence on American Freemasonry.** It is that influence which, almost without our knowing it, attaches some sort of holier-than-thou stigma to the Hour of Refreshment, frowns upon anything cheerful and festive, and gives us that grim and silent staring at a wall of which Haywood speaks. How many times have you heard a pious Brother refer sneeringly to the "Knife and Fork Mason" and to the "Six-Thirty Degree," as if there might be something reprehensible in the enjoyment of fellowship? How silly can we become? The Brethren are not going to fill the benches until the walls bulge just to see the pious Brother clown his part in the Master Mason degree, and why should they?

For some reason, Freemasonry overseas was able to escape the more dour effects of Puritanism, but on almost every facet of American life we still suffer from it. The ramifications of its influence on Freemasonry in the United States are far too numerous and controversial to discuss here, and I must not elaborate on the subject except to say that a great many of our problems today can be traced back to the period when it was deemed almost a mortal sin to eat, drink and be merry.

2. **We must remember that this is the day of the service club.** And, like it or not, our beloved Fraternity has members by the thousands who think Freemasonry should be made over to fit the Babbitt pattern; the glad-handing and first-naming, the perfunctory first stanza of "America" and the perfunctory Pledge of Allegiance, the raucous laughter, the ribald stories, the movie showing how corn plasters are manufactured. That kind of thing carried into Freemasonry becomes a travesty on Masonic fellowship, but it has crept into our Lodges, and we might as well face up to it.

3. **The casual living of our day.** By this I mean the dress of the cookout supper, the manners of the truck stop café. No Lodge can experience the true joys of the Festive Board unless the Brethren are willing to adopt some of the ways of civilization. Hard words, perhaps, but the need to be spoken.

4. **The over-emphasis on "togetherness."** (I approach the subject with fear and trembling.) Togetherness is to be encouraged, but it can be carried too far, and has been carried too far in Freemasonry. In characteristic Midwestern style, we have gone overboard. Instead of inviting the ladies' auxiliaries and the junior divisions to meet in our quarters and pursuing our own ways with dignity and restraint, we have literally abdicated in

favor of the "family" idea. Masonic fellowship has been one of the casualties.

II

Then where do we go from here?

1. **Well, first of all, we need to regain a sense of balance.** For many Masons, fellowship is the most precious jewel in the Masonic diadem. It is necessary to the very existence of our Fraternity. If Brethren can not find it in their Ancient Craft Lodge, they will find it elsewhere, and the officers and workers who howl to high heaven when new members desert their Lodge in favor of appendant organizations might reflect on the fact that the Brethren simply may be in search of that which the Lodge denies them. We need to cultivate Masonic fellowship with all our zeal – not to choke it out with trivialities, nor speak of it with supercilious scorn. We need the Hour of Refreshment in all its beauty and dignity; we need to revive those noble old traditions of our Craft. We haven't outgrown them; we haven't found anything better; we have lost something and haven't discovered what is wrong!

2. **But if the Festive Board is to serve its purpose, it must be dignified.** I have said it before and I repeat: A Masonic gathering is neither the proper time nor place for dirty language or suggestive stories. And just as lacking in propriety is the sectarian preaching, and the rabble-rousing, and the political speech disguised as "Americanism."

3. **The Festive Board must be appropriate.** It is not an occasion for comedians, nor variety shows, nor vaudeville troupes, nor tap dancers, nor magicians, nor barbershop quartets, nor homegrown movies, nor cute little child entertainers. They have their place, but their place is at the Family Night party, not at the Festive Board of Freemasonry. We can not realize the by-products of Masonic fellowship when the stage setting is so inappropriate as to be ridiculous.

4. **And finally, the Festive Board must be Masonic.** Repeatedly I am invited to Lodge banquets to deliver an address. "Give us one of those straight-from-the-shoulder Masonic speeches," they tell me in advance. "We want you to lay it right on the line." And then, lo and behold, when I arrive to deliver that so-called Masonic speech and "lay it on the line" to the Brethren, I find the room half filled with ladies and children! Bless 'em – I love them, too. But let's acknowledge the most basic of all basic fundamentals: Freemasonry is for Freemasons. Surely a few occasions

can be set aside in the annual program of

a Lodge when Master Masons can enjoy the fellowship to which they are entitled in a manner consistent with the traditions and practices of our ancient Craft.

I hope to see the day when the Table Lodge is authorized in Indiana, as it has been in the older Jurisdictions for two centuries and more. I hope to see the day when every Lodge takes pride in an appropriate observance of the Feasts of the Sts. John – something more imaginative than the tedious routine of the Master Mason degree with doughnuts and coffee afterwards! Yes, and I hope to see the day when a Master Mason in the United States will have occasion to sing of his Lodge with the same depth of feeling that Robert Burns felt when he sang of his:

Oft have I met your social band,

And spent the cheerful festive night; Oft, honor'd with supreme command, Presided o'er the sons of light; And, by that hieroglyphic bright, Which none but Craftsmen ever saw! Strong mem'ry on my heart shall write Those happy scenes, when far away.

Chapter 9
Bread or a Stone?

Question 8: What has become of that "course of moral instruction, veiled in allegory and illustrated by symbols," that Freemasonry is supposed to be?

A young man in his late twenties had just been elected Master of his Lodge. Determined to take the admonition to give "good and wholesome instruction" seriously, he ordered a copy of Carl H. Claudy's *The Master's Book*. It became his "volume of sacred law"; he literally slept with it under his pillow. These three sentences in the little book impressed him so much he underlined them in red ink.

"One thing and only one thing a Masonic Lodge can give its members which they can get nowhere else in the world. *That one thing is Masonry.* ... The Master whose instruction program is strictly Masonic has to send to the basement for extra chairs for most of his meetings."

The young fellow tried it, and it worked. It was a thrilling experience for him to see Masons who hadn't been in Lodge for years coming back regularly for Light and more Light and further Light. Nothing in 25 years has changed his conviction that the Claudy formula will fill the benches with regularity. He is still around, by the way, though not quite so youthful. I see him every morning in the mirror when I shave.

Now, no one could have known less about adult education. All the equipment I had was a little imagination and a resolute purpose to avoid schoolroom methods. Remembering the impact of teaching by means of symbols, parables, allegories and legends, we ruled out long-winded lectures; we did not lure the Brethren with stunts or vaudeville entertainment; we did not take advantage of a captive audience because the audience was not captive – the Brethren came because they wanted to. And we had to send out for extra chairs, just as Claudy said we would.

Come to think about it, has not the Master of every Lodge an obligation to give the Craft good and wholesome instruction?

Let us proceed on the assumption that every candidate for the degrees sincerely desires the Light Freemasonry has to offer him, and expects to receive it. What happens?

Well, first, we recite, recite, recite until there is nothing left to recite. Then we try to persuade the new Brother to recite also, and if memorizing and reciting do not appeal to him, we have nothing further to offer. We wash our hands of him. Disappointed, he hears that other organizations elaborate on the three degrees, and he turns to them to obtain a substitute for that which his Lodge should have provided.

He asks for bread; we give him a stone.

Admittedly there is a weakness somewhere. But where?

Respectfully I suggest we are weak: (1) in Form, and (2) in Substance.

And just as respectfully I submit that we fall short (1) at the Grand Lodge level where the designs are placed on the trestleboard, and (2) at the Lodge level where the designs are executed.

Obviously the ramifications of the subject are too great to discuss at length. I can only plant the seed.

I. In The Sanctum Sanctorum

Let's face it, then:

1. **The Word.** The very term Masonic Education is a liability – a frightening word suggestive of impractical theories and dull abstractions. What a blessing it would be if some creative soul could coin another: Masonic Light, or Advancement, or Instruction would be an improvement.

2. **Our Designs.** There are too many systems too hastily conceived, too much running wildly hither and yon in search of bright ideas. We pursue Masonic educational systems in the same manner that teen-agers pursue fads. Let a bright idea be advanced in one Jurisdiction and a score of Grand Masters will cry, "Lo, it is here!" Like sheep they rush to follow

the bellwether. And why? If Freemasonry is universal, do we need "57 Varieties" of instruction programs? After all, Master Masons respond in much the same manner the nation over.

3. **Our Architects.** They are too amateurish. An effective program for further Light can not be designed by whoever happen to be officers of a Grand Lodge in a given year. It is a job for men with special talents. Always there should be one or two men with down-to-earth experience in adult education; a public relations man to interpret human likes and dislikes; a newspaper man to tell the story in everyday English. And all should be thoroughly grounded in the fundamentals of Freemasonry.

4. **Our Working Tools.** One of the marks of an amateur writer or speaker is that he attempts to tell everything he knows each time he writes or speaks. With rare exceptions, the printed materials for Masonic education programs are like that. They insist on telling everything. Forbidding in length and appalling in scope, they are too ponderous, too dull, too windy. Ever hear of the Tractarians? We could well emulate their example.

II. In The Quarries

Again, let's face it:

1. **Our Unfinished Labors.** By and large, instruction is not a part of the program in the average Lodge. Such efforts as may be made are sporadic, conceived as an afterthought, treated as a stepchild. We have not caught fire with the possibilities, for we are so obsessed with question-and-answer memory work that we think all instruction begins and ends in a catechism. Nothing could be further from the truth.

2. **Many Are Exceedingly Anxious.** We know not the meaning of patience. When we do attempt to provide good and wholesome instruction, we try to do too much too rapidly. A first-grader is not handed a set of books which will tell him all he needs to know for a high school diploma. Rarely is a young Mason a Ninety-Day Wonder, yet when we instruct at all, we give him huge doses, without regard to his needs, likes or dislikes, and we expect them to do the work of a Vitamin B-12 shot. It isn't that simple.

3. **Rubbish In The Temple.** Regrettably, too many of our programs are tied to stunts and cheap entertainment used as bait. Masonic teaching must be Masonic or it is of no avail. We defeat the purpose when we insult the intelligence of the man who seeks.

III. Winding Stairs

Then where do we start?

1. **Most important of all, Masonic Light must come from the East.** Instruction provided by a teacher who knows less than his pupil is neither good nor wholesome. "If the blind lead the blind, both shall fall in the ditch."

It has long been my contention that the place to insist upon proficiency is in the man who wears the hat and holds the gavel. If that means minimum standards, training courses, written and oral examinations, then let's have them. I would have made a much better Master if I had had that kind of preparation.

2. **Our approach must be an intelligent one.** The program must have diversity, the doses must be small, and it must avoid dullness as a plague. Men of high intellectual attainments should have study clubs; those of limited academic training should have "capsules," and for those in the wide range in between, the possibilities are unlimited.

3. **Instruction must be lifted to a place of honor and respectability in Lodge affairs.** Above all, it should be geared to the Hour of Refreshment – not to the lecture room nor the graduate seminar. Let self-improvement become a

privilege to be enjoyed, and not a chore to be endured.

4. **We need to discard about nine-tenths of our curriculum materials.** Masonic authors whose works are authoritative and have human interest appeal could be numbered almost on the fingers of one hand. With profound apologies to local writers and compilers in every State, I maintain we could do better to stick to the classics.

5. **Any program of further Light must be pursued continuously and with infinite patience.** The parable of the Sower always should be the theme. Even though great quantities of seed will be wasted, some will take root and bear fruit – and that some is worth all the effort.

6. **And then, humbly begging pardon of the Sacred Cows, if Plans and Programs and Systems there must be, there is only one which has stood the test of time.** It is that which is carried on within the framework of the Lodge, inside its four walls, by its authority, under its control and responsible to it. Nothing should be left to whim or fancy of individuals who may be ill prepared, inaccurate or irresponsible. Textbooks, manuals, short courses, schools, forums – these should not operate as substitutes for the work of a Lodge. We can only hope that such tools may assist and

inspire. But the stones must be hewn and squared in the quarries where they are raised.

Visionary? Impossible of attainment? Of course it is. The Temple within the hearts of men is never finished. No one has suggested that the building of human character is a quick and easy job.

Who among us has faith to "lay his course by a star which he has never seen, to dig by the divining rod for springs he may never reach?"

Chapter 10
Bring the Line Up to the Standard

Question 9: Hasn't the so-called Century of the Common Man contributed to making our Fraternity a little too common?

An old legend which comes to us from the Napoleonic Wars tells of a youth, too young to fight, who was permitted to carry the regimental banner. During one bitter engagement his unit was advancing on the enemy under heavy fire. In his youthful zeal the boy went so far ahead of the regiment that he was almost out of contact. The commanding officer send a runner bearing the message, "Bring the standard back to the line."

With heroic recklessness the lad sent back the ringing reply, "Bring the line up to the standard."

In the United States today, politicians like to refer to the present age as the "Century of the Common Man." Even though no man considers himself common and every man desires mightily that his sons be uncommon men, it does make a good vote-catching phrase.

Trouble is, in our solicitous concern for the Common Man, we overlook an important principle of applied psychology. Too much emphasis on common men and common things can serve to make common that which should be uncommon. There is in evidence today what might be called for lack of a better term a Masonic Gresham's Law. Under its operations we are not thrilled with the sight of the line being brought up to the standard; instead, we witness the sad spectacle of the standard being dragged back to the line.

Whether we like it or not, let's face it. The trend is in the direction of altering the pattern to fit the cloth. It has left its mark on every Lodge in Indiana, large and small.

In bringing the subject out into the open, I am not merely unburdening myself of a personal irritation – I am only putting into print what has been whispered in my ear on countless occasions these last 15 years.

When we cease to set a lofty mark and expect our Brethren to measure up to it, when we permit a downward adjustment to conform to practices and manners that are casual and lax and crude, we are dealing our beloved Fraternity a double blow:

First, a blow from without. Certainly we must not expect to retain the prestige the Craft has enjoyed in the past if we can lift our sights no higher than the bowling lanes, the drive-in hamburger stand, the picnic grounds.

Second, a blow from within. Will not men respect and venerate Freemasonry more if they know there are certain rules of gentility – of behavior, of dress, of speech and decorum – which they are expected to observe?

What am I talking about? All right, then, let's spell it out:

1. **The appearance and actions of Master Masons in public ceremonies.** Not always do they create a favorable impression. Only on rare occasions may Freemasons perform their ritualistic work outside the Lodge hall, usually a funeral or the laying of a cornerstone. It requires no great degree of imagination to see what damage can be done the entire Fraternity when men do not possess that priceless gift known as "a sense of the fitness of things."

One time I attended the funeral rites for a beloved Brother. At the conclusion of the church service the Brethren filed down the center aisle in view of all in attendance to take their places in the escort. The bearer of the Three Great Lights did not know what to do with his head gear. So, down the aisle went the procession with a faded straw hat on top of the Holy Bible, Square and Compass.

What am I talking about? Aprons that are crumpled and soiled. Whether worn without the Lodge room or within, the apron itself is disgraced when it is anything less than spotless, and the Fraternity is cheapened, to say nothing of the psychological effect upon the wearer himself.

Yes, and I am talking about the ridiculous spectacle of the Master Mason who appears anywhere with long apron strings dangling from the rear, all too suggestive of the limp tail of an old white cow I used to know. Must we go out of our way to make ourselves a laughing stock?

2. **Then there are the coarse and boorish performances by self-appointed comedians, and by the Glue Factory Craft Club, in conferring**

the Master Mason degree. I have seen the Sublime Degree lose all its sublimity in a matter of seconds when immature men forfeited their opportunity to convey a never-to-be-forgotten lesson and chose instead to show off like little boys. On my private black list are the names of Lodges in which I simply choose not be present when the Master Mason degree is conferred. Some of them, I am sorry to say, are in Indiana. Twenty-four years ago Carl H. Claudy was saying the same thing in a Short Talk Bulletin which the Master of every Lodge would do well to obtain and read again and again.

3. **Finally, let's lay it on the line. I am talking about the lack of respect shown by the Masons for their Lodge as reflected in the attire they wear to its meetings.** It was Past Master's Night. An invited guest, I sat on the sidelines to witness the always pleasant conferring of the Sublime Degree by those veterans who had borne the heat and burden of the day.

At first all went well. The ritual that only Past Masters know was executed as only Past Masters can. Then King Solomon approached the East. The man who represented that wise and noble ruler wore a slouch felt hat a half-size too large that caused his ears to droop forward. Coatless, his loud pattered sport shirt was buttoned at the throat without benefit of a necktie. Taking his place in the oriental chair, he laid the heel of a yellow right shoe on his left knee, and began chewing his gum thoughtfully.

"Even Solomon in all his glory," I mused to myself, "was not arrayed like one of these."

Yes, I know the subject of a man's personal appearance is a touchy one. Nevertheless, I stoutly maintain that appropriate dress for Masons while attending meetings of their Lodge simply is not a debatable issue. A Lodge hall is dedicated in the name of Jehovah. It is set apart as a place in which the Great Architect of the Universe is an object of our reverence. Why, then, should there be any question about proper and respectful attire in the Lodge room any more than the Church?

Recently a distinguished officer of the Grand Lodge of California prepared a most effective pamphlet under the title, *If Freemasonry Is Good, Let Us Talk About It.* This one paragraph deserves frequent repetition: "The Mason who creates a bad impression, in whatever field of activity, can bring discredit to the Craft. I am in the women's clothing business, and in our business we are concerned about what our female employees wear 'off the job' as well as on. Our salesgirls make an impression at all times – and we want it to be a good impression."

Let us not cloud the issue with pious mouthings about how Masonry regards no man for his worldly wealth and honors; that it is the internal and not the external qualifications of a man that render him worthy to be a Mason. The question is not one of honors – it is of respect for the dignity of our ancient Craft. Mark it down: *If the internal qualifications are there some of those qualifications will show through on the outer side.* A Mason need not wear a Hart, Schaffner & Marx suit to show proper respect for his Lodge, but certainly there should be a high point below which even laziness and negligence will not permit him to descend.

Sometimes I wonder what a serious minded young Mason must think when he looks about the Lodge room and sees his Brethren attired as they would for an outdoor steak fry. Does his mind go back to the time when he received his preliminary instructions prior to initiation as an Entered Apprentice? Perhaps he recalls two significant sentences: "Put on your freshest and most immaculate garments," he was told, "that their spotless cleanliness may be symbolic of the faultless purity of your intentions. With your body clean and your garments spotless you are more suitably prepared to receive that spotless and faultless philosophy which Masonry will offer you."

Yes, perhaps the young Mason *does* remember those sentences. He may be one of the sizable army of newly raised Brethren that drift away from their Lodges never to return!

All these practices and many more serve to cheapen Freemasonry in the eyes of the public and in the eyes of the Brethren themselves.

Much more could and should be said. For example, my criticism has been confined to the Symbolic Lodge. But the Symbolic Lodge does not stand alone in the cheapening process, by any means. Organizations which restrict their membership to Masons and which profit by their relationship to the Craft are doing their part rather well in dragging the standard back to the line.

Now let there be no defensive bleating that the Grand Secretary has gone over to the silk stocking crowd and is promoting tea parties. The choice is not bowling league attire versus white tie and tails. I only insist that Masons, of all persons, should have that fine "sense of the fitness of things;" a wholesome respect for the Lodge and the place it should occupy in the lives of men; the same kind of respect a man should show his church when he goes to worship, or the family of a friend when he attends a wedding, or his host when he is invited to Thanksgiving dinner. Just plain good taste, that's all.

Will the Brethren complain if Lodges insist on dignity, decorum, respect? Will interest lag, attendance fall, membership decline?

Well, take a look at interest and attendance and membership *now.*

When good men are summoned to the highest and best within them, they usually respond with the highest and best. We might be pleasantly surprised at the reaction of our Brethren if challenged to bring the line up to the standard where it belongs!

Chapter 11
Let's Try Freemasonry

Question 10: Are there not too many well-meaning Brethren who are working overtime to make Freemasonry something other than Freemasonry?

"Whither are we traveling?" was my anxious query ten months ago, and there followed ten searching questions on subjects that have disturbed me increasingly in recent years.

With the promise of a series of articles in which each subject would be explored, I added:

"I shall propose no bright new ideas – not one. All I am going to advocate is that Freemasonry remain Freemasonry; and if we have strayed from the traditional path, we had better be moving back to the main line while there is yet time to restore the prestige and respect, the loyalty and devotion that once was ours."

Thus was notice served at the outset that I would not be found aligned with anyone who seeks to make Freemasonry over and bring it up-to-date that it will be out-of-date tomorrow.

I

In all the land there is weeping and wailing and gnashing of teeth. The Masonic Gimmick Manufacturing Company, Unlimited, is working overtime to devise stunts to "modernize" Freemasonry, to put it in line with ten thousand other organizations that clamor for the attention of the Tribal American. Among its many products we are urged to try these:

• Abandon the "free will and accord" rule which has placed our Craft far above the mine run of societies, and permit outright solicitation.
• Ape the service clubs. Get busy on "projects" galore in the best

Babbitt fashion.

• Go into the organized do-good business in a big way. Find an area of the human body that has not been exploited. Exploit it. Set a quota, have a kick-off dinner, ring the doorbells.

• Subsidize other organizations right and left, and, in the doing, ignore, neglect and starve the parent body.

• Feminize the Fraternity. Carry "togetherness" to even more ridiculous extremes than we have already.

• Hire press agents to tell the world, like Little Jack Horner, what great boys we are. ("Masonry is not getting its proper share of publicity," complains one Grand Master.) Never mind actions; concentrate on words.

• Imitate Hollywood. Stage an extravaganza. Bring in all the groups that ever fancied themselves remotely related to Freemasonry. Form the parade, blow the bugle, beat the drums and cheapen the Fraternity.

• Let Freemasonry "take a position" on public issues of the day. Stand up and be counted (assuming, of course, that the position the Craft takes is in line with our own pet prejudices.)

• Go all out for materialism. Raise money; spend it. Build temples, institutions. Subsidize; endow. Whatever can be had by writing a check, get it.

• Centralize, centralize, centralize. Pattern Freemasonry after Washington bureaucracy. Let nothing be done modestly by an individual or a Lodge; do everything on state or national level the super-duper way. Make a great to-do about local self-government, but accept no local self-responsibility.

Why does not someone suggest that we try Freemasonry?

Certainly we haven't been trying it these many years. We have experimented with just about everything the mind of man (and of woman) can imagine. Why not get back to our knitting?

II

Looking at the overall picture of American Masonry candidly and thoughtfully, it seems to me the greatest single need of our Craft today is a membership with a better understanding of what our Fraternity is and especially of what it is not.

Few indeed are the Master Masons who know what Freemasonry really is; even more rare is the species with a comprehension of what Freemasonry is not. Seniority and rank seem to have little relationship to our ignorance. The number of Masters, Past Masters and Grand Masters who are hazy as to what our Craft is all about is appalling.

What has happened?

Well, we seem to assume that Freemasonry is a fly-by-night fad of the mid-Twentieth Century; something to be tossed hither and yon by every wind that blows. In the restless, superficial age in which we live, we are impatient unless our organized bodies have slogans, and carry banners, and make official pronouncements on every subject under the sun, however trivial. We want them to follow the conventional pattern; to maintain lobbies, to publish aims and objectives, conduct drives and campaigns, strive to get into the headlines and on the airwaves, write checks to everything that sounds benevolent and has a board of directors, and, in general, to have a finger in every pie.

Freemasonry does none of these.

Strange, is it not, that our ancient Craft should have gained for itself such a preeminent position of honor and prestige when it does almost nothing in the conventional manner!

III

Then *what is this Freemasonry* to which I urge our Brethren to return? What are its aims and objectives? What does it do?

Perhaps the last place we would expect to find an answer would be in the First Book of Kings, and even then the answer will come as something of a disappointment, for it is all so different from the ways to which we have become accustomed.

Elijah was languishing in his cave on Mount Horeb in the conviction that of all God's children only he had remained faithful to his trust. By divine command, Elijah went forth and stood upon the mountain, and the prophet tells us what happened:

"And behold, the Lord passed by, and a great and strong wind rent the mountains, and brake in pieces the rocks before the Lord; but the Lord was not in the wind: and after the wind an earthquake; but the Lord was not in the earthquake: and after the earthquake a fire; but the Lord was not in the fire: and after the fire a still small voice."

What does this mean to us this day? It means that Freemasonry erects its temples within the hearts of men. Even though we may not understand what we are saying, we sound forth our purpose in trumpet tones when, in our own Declaration of Principles, we proclaim,

"Through the improvement and strengthening of the character of the individual man, Freemasonry seeks to improve the community."

And we tell the candidate for the degrees of Masonry the same thing in words striking in their simplicity. *"The design of the Masonic Institution,"* we say to him, *"is to make its votaries wiser, better, and consequently happier."* Not a word about mass action, nor pressure groups, nor resolutions on matters of state policy. No "pro" this or "anti" that. No sales talk for any pet scheme. No great undertakings to cure the ills of the world by making everyone over to fit a pattern of our own design. No running about like chickens with their heads cut off in search of a do-good project with which to gain favorable notice. No restless biting of the nails to compete with a service club or a civic league. No endless "busyness" which loses sight of the objective.

The message of Freemasonry? Just this: that the Lord is not to be found in the wind, nor in the earthquake, nor in the fire, but in the still, small voice!

The purpose of Freemasonry? Its purpose is the same as it has been since the day when the stones for King Solomon's Temple were hewn, squared and numbered in the quarries where they were raised. It is to take an individual – just one man at a time, mind you, and as good a man as possible – and try to make a better man out of him. That is all. How desperately the world needs just that! And if that technique is outmoded, then the experience of two thousand years is all wrong; the Parable of the Mustard Seed is horse-and-buggy philosophy; the Leaven in the Loaf is a cruel hoax.

The mere fact that men do not comprehend its purpose does not mean that Freemasonry has no purpose, nor that its purpose is outmoded – it only means that the stones are not being well hewn and squared in the quarries where they are raised.

Freemasonry has not been tried in the balance and found wanting: it has been found difficult and not tried.

More than anything else today, the world yearns for that same kind of gentle, healing influence at work in the hearts of men. The Masonic Institution, which is sometimes looked upon with scorn because it does not operate in the conventional manner, is prepared to bear witness to the fact that the conventional way of our age leaves much to be desired, and to stand upon its own majestic affirmation that the way to change human systems is to change human lives.

The wise and venerable Dean Roscoe Pound has seen more of life than most of us, and views history with greater philosophical calm, perhaps, than any of us. Here is his message to the Brethren of the Craft: *"Freemasonry has more to offer the Twentieth Century than the Twentieth Century has to offer Freemasonry."*

Whither, then, are we traveling?

I come to the conclusion of this series of exploratory articles with my faith in the basic worth of our ancient Craft unshaken, convinced that *the solution to Freemasonry's problems is Freemasonry.*

Why do we not try it?

EVOLUTION OF THE RITUAL
by Naresh Sharma, P.M.

Masonry Gets Organized

How was the somewhat confused history of the building industry, the trade regulations, and the moral precepts of Operative Masons, together with rather crude usage and phrases associated with the imparting the Mason Word, modified and elaborated as ultimately to justify the claim of Freemasonry to be a peculiar system of morality, veiled in allegory and illustrated by symbols? It is a long journey of very wise ancestors whose names we may never know, and their wisdom to make Masonry relevant and meaningful to the times in which they lived.

In June 1717 four London lodges met to form a Grand Lodge. At this time it was a radical concept introduced into Masonry. Masonry had only two degrees, that of the Entered Apprentice and Fellow of the Craft. There was no ritual, no laws for governance or edicts, by-laws, constitutions, or jurisdiction. It took almost the rest of the eighteenth century for most of this to happen. The Grand Lodge was formed and they met quarterly, but no minutes of these meetings were kept until 1723 when Rev. Anderson presented the first set of Constitutions. Brother George Bell was a Deputy Grand Master in 1751 and had not progressed beyond the degree of Fellow Craft.

Let us see what some of the practices were in those early days of organized Masonry. Lodges governed themselves by the "Old Charges" or the "Manuscript Constitutions" dating from the Regius Manuscript, c. 1390. About 130 of the Old Charges have been found, the last was found in 1954 and is called the Kevan MS, c. 1714. More than 75 of these documents are dated before 1717. Of the Old Charges, most are preserved in England and Scotland, four are in US (Boston and Philadelphia) and one is in Canada.

The Old Charges can be divided into eight distinct families but they all followed a general pattern, which was:

a. Opening prayer.
b. A reading of the legendary history of the Craft going back to Biblical times.

This was fabricated history, but it provided a traditional background for long standing customs. These histories contained

Charges, singular and general, designed to preserve and elevate the moral character of the Craftsmen.

    c.   Code of Moral and Trade Regulation.

    d.   Oath or obligation.

    e.   Arrangements for Annual Assemblies.

    f.   Procedure for Admission of New Members.

    g.   Procedure for Trial and Punishment.

Petition, Investigation, and Ballotting

There were no petitions, committees, or balloting on candidates. Names were recommended member; those present discussed the merits of the candidate and agreed to admit him in the Craft. There was no waiting time before a degree was conferred and no interval between the first and second degrees, in fact the Fellow Craft degree was conferred on the same evening. It was mandated in 1777 that the Entered Apprentice and Fellow Craft degrees be conferred on different evenings.

Making a Mason

The first evidence of two degrees is found in 1598. It is in 1725 that we find the first evidence of a Master Mason Degree. Early lodges met in taverns only for the purpose of making masons. The admission ceremony was in the form of a feast and was the same for the Apprentice and Fellow Craft. It consisted of an opening prayer followed by a reading of appropriate charges and regulations. Then the candidate took his oath, which was declaring his fidelity to the King, to the Master, Craft, and a promise that he would obey the regulations and not bring shame to the Craft. There were no penalties in these oaths. It was in 1593, according to the Grand Lodge No.1 MS, the third oldest of the Old Charges, we find the words, « one of the elders would hold out the Bible and he or they that are to be admitted shall place their hand thereon. " The word secrecy was first found in the Edinburgh Register House MS, c. 1696." We also find that the obligation of the first and second degree was the same, the only difference was three words. The words, "without equivocation or mental reservation" first appear in Sloane MS, c. 1700. Penalties are first noticed in Dumfries No. 4 MS, c. 1710, where it says, "my heart taken out alive, my head cut off, my body buried within ye sea mark."

At this time the penalties were not part of the obligation, but were included in the ritual that followed the oath. The Grand Mystery of Freemasons Discovered, c. 1724 and Wilkinson's MS, c. 1727, but found in 1946, are found the words "….and help and assist any brother as far as your ability will allow. .."

The Entered Apprentice obligation in 1727 follows the present form. The Master Mason obligation in Three Distinct Knocks, c. 1760, consists of only five paragraphs. In 1760, the penalties in the obligation are separated. It is quite clear that the admission ceremonies until the 1760's were brief, not performed in any set form of words/ritual except in the obligation, and that the theory and principles of the Order were subsequently conveyed to the novices through non-standardised lectures that brothers gave or read. During the latter part of the eighteenth century the ceremonies became more elaborate and took on the form that we know today. The ritualises that made the greatest impact on this transformation during the period of enlightenment were: William Hutchinson, Roland Calcott, and William Preston. Hutchinson philosophised and symbolised the ritual. Calcott improved on that and became the first of the "roving lecturers" teaching the lectures etc. He came to the US and among his pupils were Robert Livingston, Paul Revere, and Joseph Warren. He is credited with introducing "moral and social virtues" in the closing prayer, "subdue their passions and improve themselves in Masonry" and "it is the internal and not the external qualifications that make a man a Mason." Nobody had a greater influence than William Preston in England and Thomas Smith Webb in America. Today all Grand Lodges in the US, except Pennsylvania that follows the Irish form, follow the Preston-Webb form of lectures and ritual.

Obligation and Penalties

Dumfries MS, c. 1710. I quote the oath, "The charges we now rehearse to you with all other charges and secrets otherwise belonging to free masons or any that enter their interest for curiosity together with the counsels of this holy lodge chamber, you shall not for any gift, bribe, or reward favor, or affection directly or indirectly, nor for any cause whatsoever divulge, disclose the same to either father, mother, sister, brother, children, stranger, or any other person whatsoever, so help you God."

In the charge that followed the oath, the candidate was admonished not to take another fellow's wife, daughter, or maid in adultery or fornication. He was urged to visit the sick, relieve the poor, not to steal, and not to call other masons disrespectful names. The candidate was directed to be true to God, the Holy Catholic Church, the King and his master.

Oath in the Grand Myetery of Free Masons Discovered, c. 1724.

I quote, "You must serve God according to the best of your knowledge and institution, and be a true liege man to the king and help and assist any brother as far as your ability will allow.

By the contents of this sacred writ you will perform this oath. So help you God." THERE IS STILL ONLY ONE OATH FOR BOTH DEGREES, NO PENALTIES ARE INCLUDED AND NO SPECIFIC POSTURE OF TAKING THE OATH.

It is in 1760 that a separate obligation appears for each degree and each obligation has integral to it its penalty. During this period we also find formalised opening and closing ceremonies, preparations of candidates in different degrees, symbolised working tools, presentation of apron in degrees, circumambulation ceremony for calling the lodge from labor to refreshment. The first evidence of a lecture on charity is in the 1770's and we find the traditional third degree history lecture at about the same time.

Practices in Louisiana in the Nineteenth Century

I learned that lodges conducted all the business in the Entered Apprentice Degree in Louisiana until the union of the two Grand Lodges in 1850. The first recorded examination of a candidate was in 1850. In 1812, the Grand Lodge of Louisiana ordered its constituent lodges to procure three copies of the ritual from the Grand Secretary. In 1823, our Grand Lodge was opened in New Orleans in the Entered Apprentice Degree to receive General Lafayette who visited as a Guest of the Nation.

Conclusion

The ritual that we have inherited has undergone countless changes in the last three hundred years. Wise men made changes as they thought were needed. The practices in the lodge have changed continuously over the centuries. Then why do we suspect our leaders today that advocate changes? Brethren, let us support our leadership so Masonry can keep moving ahead.

JAMES FOULHOUZE
A Biographical Study
by Michael R. Poll, P.M.
Secretary, Louisiana Lodge of Research

Mr. Pike is altogether unknown to me, and I have never seen him, which is perhaps to be regretted, because in the event he spoke to me pursuant to the information which he has received from ill- disposed individuals, I suppose that he will be sorry for having allowed his pen to write what is neither correct nor rational.

- James Foulhouze, 1858.[1]

James Foulhouze was, unquestionably, the arch-nemesis of Albert Pike in Pike's early days as Grand Commander of the Supreme Council, Southern Jurisdiction, USA. Judge James Foulhouze, former Roman Catholic priest, Sovereign Grand Inspector General of the Grand Orient of France and Sovereign Grand Commander of the Supreme Council of Louisiana in the pre-Concordat of 1855 period along with some of the leading New Orleans Masons, including the very respected Judge T. Wharton Collens and the powerful United States Senator Pierre Soulé, may have nearly destroyed the concordat between the New Orleans and Charleston Supreme Councils - a concordat which was the breath of life to the newly reorganized Charleston Supreme Council. Who was this man who could have caused such a disturbance ? *Did* he cause the disturbance or was he, himself, swept along in a tidal wave of events?

The following is a glimpse into the life and tumultuous Masonic times of a most significant, but highly controversial, figure in the history of the US Scottish Rite. It is to be regretted that no photograph or likeness of Foulhouze is known to exist. It is, also, unfortunate that some areas of his life are simply lost in the mists of time.

On 1 October 1800,[2] Jacques Foulhouze was born to Michel and Jeanne Cronier Foulhouze in Riom, France. The young Foulhouze received a Catholic education at the Seminary of St. Sulpice in Paris culminating in his ordination as a Roman Catholic priest. The Reverend James Foulhouze traveled to the United States and labored in the Diocese of Philadelphia in 1834 and 35.[3] The next found record concerning Foulhouze in the US comes in 1835 when his name appears in a Philadelphia court records book of aliens declaring their intention to take the oath of allegiance to the United States.[4] Foulhouze would not long remain a priest nor keep his domicile in Philadelphia. An 1858 New Orleans publication contains interesting comments about Foulhouze and his possible reasons for leaving the priesthood. The comments were written by Charles Laffon de Ladébat, a leading figure in mid 19th century New Orleans Scottish Rite Masonry, who will be discussed further later in this paper. Ladébat says that Foulhouze might have remained a priest had not, "Mr. (now bishop) Hughes been appointed, *in his stead*, to the important rector ship of a northern parish, to which Mr. Foulhouze was, for his long service, justly entitled."[5]

John Hughes (1797-1864) was the fourth bishop and first Archbishop of the Roman Catholic diocese of New York. Hughes served with Foulhouze in the Diocese of Philadelphia and founded there the *Catholic Herald* newspaper. Hughes was consecrated coadjutor to Bishop John Dubois of New York in 1838. He succeeded Dubois in 1842 and became archbishop of New York in 1850.[6] Foulhouze, regardless of Ladébat's comments, could not have been affected by the 1838 Hughes appointment as the *Journal Notes* of Philadelphia Bishop Francis Kenrick record Foulhouze's faculties being suspended on 5 February 1836.[7] As with many areas of Foulhouze's life, it is unclear what could have taken place causing his separation from the priesthood. Foulhouze was a graduate of the highly respected Seminary of St. Sulpice. Many Catholic dioceses consider such graduates to be a highly desirable prize. The accounts of Foulhouze for that time, however, tell a different story. The records of the Archdiocese of Philadelphia,[8] while confirming that Foulhouze was, indeed, a priest assigned to them, show had he had "no specific assignment."[9] This is an interesting situation. Why would the Diocese of Philadelphia not take advantage of the quality education that Foulhouze received by putting his abilities and education to use? Foulhouze, himself, may provide the answer. In 1843 Foulhouze was asked if he had taken the vows of the priesthood, he replied: "No, but it is true that they were given to me, against my will."[10] Regardless of the philosophical point Foulhouze was trying to make, his statement reflects that he may not have ever wholly embraced the priesthood. If Foulhouze's work reflected the same lack of interest, then it is very likely that regardless of what seminary he attended, he would not have been given assignments nor appointments to higher positions. All conjecture aside, Foulhouze did leave the priesthood, pursue a career in law and move to New Orleans.

Foulhouze began his law career in Philadelphia after leaving the priesthood. In 1842, he published a book in Philadelphia that reflected the same interest in philosophy that was maintained throughout his life. The 200 page work was titled, *A Philosophical Inquiry Respecting the Abolition of Capital Punishment*.[11] It is possible that Foulhouze was in New Orleans when this book was released, but it is clear that he was in New Orleans the following year. Philadelphia Bishop Francis Kenrick (Foulhouze's former superior) writes in a 1843 letter:

> Here affairs go on smoothly but at New Orleans an infidel faction are struggling to destroy or subjugate the Episcopal authority. A fallen French priest, Foulhouze, is the editor of an impious paper,[12] the organ of the Marguillers. [...] The leaders in disorder are Freemasons, and they contrived to set apart a lot in the Cemetery for their Masonic brethren, and had it dedicated by a speech from their Grand Master who is a Marguiller.[13]

The Marguillers were the wardens of the St. Louis Cathedral in New Orleans. The Grand Master that Kenrick spoke of was E. A. Canon, who was not only a Marguiller, but the President of the Marguillers. The Marguillers (many of whom were Freemasons) controlled the appointments of the priests for the St. Louis Cathedral during the early to mid 1800's. There was, of course, a great division within the congregation over Freemasons having a say in the appointment of their parish priests (regardless of the fact that these Freemasons were, themselves, Roman Catholic and members of the parish). In New Orleans, Masonry and the Roman Catholic faith were tightly intertwined for a number of years in a love/hate relationship. It was a situation not without some hostile conflicts. An event that took place in 1842 is worth mentioning:

> On the feast of All Saints, an incident took place in the Cathedral which was in itself trivial, but which shows to what lengths the two factions[14] would go. While Father Jamey was preaching, E. A. Canon, the

president of the Marguillers, entered the sanctuary by way of the choir entrance, and made a tour of the altar towards that place assigned to the president of the wardens (side opposite the door of the sacristy by which he entered). He remained there for a few minutes, but not being able to hear very well, he advanced to the balustrade of a neighboring chapel, in order to hear better. He had only heard a few words, and then decided to retire by the way he had come in, that is, behind the altar. As he was going out he was greeted by Octave de Armas, a parishioner loyal to [Bishop] Blanc, (who was also seated in the sanctuary) with the words, "Get out; you are not in your place..." Canon answered this with apparent sharp disdain and was preparing to leave when he was pushed. He was near the door of the sacristy and fell on the steps. On getting up he heard Armas distinctly cry, "I, I alone will get rid of the wardens." The services were interrupted for about five minutes, but the Mass was soon continued and all ended calmly.[15]

The event may have ended "calmly" at that time, but the incident was far from over. As a result of his being pushed in the St. Louis Cathedral, Canon, following typical Creole custom, sought satisfaction from Armas by means of challenging him to a duel. Armas, however, refused the challenge on the grounds that he was a Roman Catholic.[16] Friends of Canon would not let the matter drop and charges were filed against Armas with the City Recorder. Armas was found guilty of assault. The incident is reflective of the growing tensions between the factions within the New Orleans Catholic community. It was in this atmosphere and, likely, through the contacts with the Marguillers that Foulhouze was introduced to Louisiana Masonry. It obviously attracted him and he sought to be a member.

From Priest to Freemason

The Marguillers might have introduced James Foulhouze to Louisiana Masonry, but it was not his first exposure to Freemasonry itself. Foulhouze stated in 1857:

> "Being a Grandson of Free-masons, I, in my early years, conceived and entertained a desire to enter the fraternity ..." [17]

Foulhouze fulfilled that early desire by becoming a member of *Los Amigos del Orden*, a Spanish speaking, New Orleans Scottish Rite Lodge. [18] Foulhouze also stated:

> "Within a year from my initiation I was made a Master Mason in the same Lodge." [19]

There are, unfortunately, no known records of the initiation of Foulhouze nor can an exact date be placed on his initiating, passing or raising. Foulhouze did state in his *Historical Inquiry* that he was initiated by Antonio Costa. [20] Costa was Worshipful Master of *Los Amigos del Orden* in 1843. An 1843 initiation followed by an 1844 raising meant rapid advancement for Foulhouze. Foulhouze was, apparently, viewed as a Mason of promise. On 14 February 1845 he was appointed Grand Translator by the Grand Lodge. The office of Grand Translator did not exist prior to Foulhouze receiving the appointment. The office was created due to the growing need for French to English and English to French translations in Grand Lodge records and documents.

In the summer of 1845 (about a year after Foulhouze became a Master Mason) Foulhouze traveled to France carrying a letter of introduction from Robert Preaux, Grand Master of the Grand Lodge of Louisiana and Active Member of the Supreme Council of Louisiana. During his stay in Paris, Foulhouze received all of the degrees of the A.A.S.R. culminating in the 33rd degree on 27 September from the Grand College of Rites of the Grand Orient of France. The speed in which Foulhouze received the degrees is extraordinary and certainly was not normal procedure for the Grand Orient. There is no explanation to be found as to why this very rare honor was given to such a young Master Mason nor has the contents of the letter from Preaux ever been revealed. Regardless of what activities Foulhouze later engaged in, he was, in the eyes of the U.S. Masonic community, a legitimate Sovereign Grand Inspector General. Of this event, Foulhouze comments:

The Scotch Rite [...] pleased me on account of its truly philosophical principles, and the more I studied it, the more I felt anxious to take its superior degrees, when a fair opportunity so to do offered itself to me in 1845.

I was in France, and on the recommendations and letters of my Scotch brothers here, the worshipful Lodge "Clémente Amitié" opened its door to me, and after a short stay among them I was made a Knight R:. + and a Knight Kadosh, which I am bound to say, rendered still clearer to my eyes and intellect the views which I had long entertained on the merits of the Scotch Rite, and for ever attached me to its admirable and useful tenets.

The favors thus bestowed on me, were unexpected, and I certainly desired no others, when on a special and unasked resolution of the Supreme Council in the Grand Orient, I was called and raised in that body to the thirty third degree.[21]

Following the death of Sovereign Grand Commander Jean-Jacques Conte, New Orleans Judge Jean-François Canonge, an influential Past Grand Master of the Grand Lodge of Louisiana, became the Grand Commander of the Supreme Council of Louisiana on 20 September 1845.[22] Foulhouze said of Canonge:

As long as he lived, I had but little to do, and contented myself with studying the rite ...[23]

Foulhouze, who had affiliated with the Supreme Council of Louisiana in 1846, was, regardless of his comments, not idle during this period. Foulhouze was appointed Grand Secretary of the Supreme Council of Louisiana in 1847.[24] He, also, advanced through the chairs of *Los Amigos del Orden* serving as its Worshipful Master in 1847. Once serving his term as Worshipful Master, he was elected a life member of the Grand Lodge. It must also be pointed out that the invasion of the jurisdiction of the Grand Lodge of Louisiana by the Grand Lodge of Mississippi and the creation of the Louisiana Grand Lodge in 1848 would, surely, have occupied a considerable amount of time with all the Worshipful Masters of New Orleans Lodges.

The Grand Lodge of Mississippi and the Union of 1850

A faction within the New Orleans English-speaking York Rite Masons felt that the 1844 Constitution of the Grand Lodge of Louisiana sanctioning the cumulation of the three rites worked by lodges in Louisiana (French, Scottish & York) altered the Grand Lodge into a body that was no longer a true York Rite Grand Lodge.[25] The decision was made by these Masons to sever their association with the Grand Lodge and organize themselves into what they felt was proper York Rite Masonry. A committee was formed and a letter of grievance was brought before the Grand Lodge of Mississippi on 23 January 1845.[26] The Grand Master of the Grand Lodge of Mississippi was Mexican War hero and former governor of Mississippi, John Anthony Quitman. The Grand Lodge of Mississippi appointed a committee to go to New Orleans in order to examine the situation. On 21 January 1846, the committee from the Grand Lodge of Mississippi appointed to examine the charges presented by the York Masons from New Orleans presented three reports concerning the events. The first report was presented on behalf of the majority of the committee and concluded that there was "no Grand Lodge of Ancient York Masons within the limits of the State of Louisiana" and that the Grand Lodge of Mississippi had "the power, and it is its duty on proper application, to issue Dispensations and Charters to bodies of Ancient York Masons within the limits of the State of Louisiana, until the constitution of a Grand Lodge within that State."[27] Two "counter" reports were then presented which advised against the Grand Lodge of Mississippi issuing charters within the jurisdiction of the Grand Lodge of Louisiana. The outcome of the events of 21 January (despite the efforts of the two "counter" reports) was the chartering of *George Washington* Lodge in New Orleans and *Lafayette* Lodge in Lafayette[28] by the Grand Lodge of Mississippi on 22 February. Relations were severed between the Grand Lodges of Louisiana and Mississippi. The Louisiana Lodges chartered by the Grand Lodge of Mississippi were declared irregular by the Grand Lodge of Louisiana. In total, the Grand Lodge of Mississippi chartered seven Lodges in the New Orleans area by 1848.[29] These seven Lodges united to form the "Louisiana Grand Lodge of

Ancient York Masons" on 8 March 1848. The Grand Lodge of Mississippi received admonishment from most U.S. Grand Lodges and the majority openly condemned its action.[30] While the future for this splinter group of the Grand Lodge of Louisiana may have looked bleak, several events took place to not only strengthen the position of the English-speaking New Orleans Masons, but to assure them of total victory by the loss of French control over most all forms of Louisiana Masonry.

One of the last official acts of Grand Commander Jean-François Canonge was a speech made on 3 November 1847 in Baton Rouge in which he is reported as stating that a circular issued by the Mississippi lodges in New Orleans was "unworthy of notice."[31] Canonge died on 19 January 1848. On 31 January 1848 James Foulhouze was elected Grand Commander of the Supreme Council of Louisiana. The Foulhouze election bypassed a number of senior members of the Council and, clearly, established the popularity of Foulhouze with the Council. Foulhouze had brought with him various rituals from France[32] which he edited for the New Orleans Council.[33] During the same month as the death of Canonge and the election of Foulhouze, the Charleston Council was talking an action that greatly strengthened its own position and further weakened the hold of the French-speaking New Orleans Masons. Albert Mackey (the Grand Secretary of the Charleston Council) sent a notice to the *Freemason's Monthly Magazine*[34] (Boston) which read:

> "At a special session of the Supreme Council ... for the Southern Jurisdiction of the United States of America, our Illustrious Brother, John A. Quitman ... Major General in the Army of the United States, was elected to fill a vacancy in this Supreme Council, and was duly and formally inaugurated a Sovereign Grand Inspector General of the 33d. All Consistories, Councils, Chapters and Lodges under this jurisdiction are hereby ordered to obey and respect him accordingly."[35]

On 29 January 1849 the Grand Lodge of Louisiana published a report that Foulhouze wrote for them concerning the cumulation of the rites practiced by the Grand Lodge and on 26 February the Grand Lodge published Foulhouze's report on the 1833 Concordat. Both reports upheld the positions of the Grand Lodge of Louisiana and encouraged the continued practice of the cumulation of the rites in Louisiana.

On 14 September 1849 Foulhouze, along with a several other New Orleans Masons, were honored by *Friends of Harmony* Lodge (whose Worshipful Master was elder Past Grand Master and New Orleans Supreme Council Member John Henry Holland) by being made honorary members of the lodge. An excerpt from the Minutes of the Lodge reads:

> "Whereas by their great ability and impartiality our well beloved Brethren Joseph Walker, Jas. Foulhouze, P. Willman, John D. Kemper & R. Preaux have earned the destination of Honorary Membership, their services in the Masonic vineyard entitling them to some suitable token or tribute of appreciation of their worth, and of the high respect entertained for their estimable personal and Masonic character - they being Brethren to whom a burdened may pour out his sorrows, to whom distress may prefer its suit; Brethren whose hands are guided by justice and whose hearts are expanded by benevolence.
>
> Therefore be it now decreed, that the aforesaid distinguished Brethren be and they are hereby created Honorary Members of the Friends of Harmony Lodge of F & A Masons, this as a testimony of regard for the inestimable services as Masons, and their courtesy, affability and kindness as men - well worthy of initiation and the foregoing preamble and resolution being seconded and put is carried unanimously. [36]

The Union of 1850

The 1848 Louisiana Grand Lodge obtained recognition from only one other Grand Lodge — the Grand Lodge of Mississippi. In 1849 John Gedge, a New Orleans attorney, was elected Grand Master of the Louisiana Grand Lodge. Despite what would seem to be the irregularity of the Louisiana Grand Lodge and the lack of support for this new Grand Lodge within the Masonic community, the Grand

Lodge of Louisiana entered into negotiations and finally merged with this body in 1850. The Grand Lodge of Louisiana was left with little choice in this matter. The fact that the Grand Lodge of Louisiana was overwhelmingly considered the "regular" Grand Lodge was not sufficient to overcome the internal problems stemming from the cultural divisions in New Orleans. By mid 1849, it was likely realized that the English-speaking lodges which had remained loyal to the Grand Lodge were showing signs that continued loyalty would, most likely, not happen. Obviously realizing that the total collapse of the Grand Lodge of Louisiana was a very real possibility, the Grand Lodge of Louisiana and the Louisiana Grand Lodge entered into talks designed to merge the two bodies.[37] That merger took place in June of 1850 with the approval of a new Constitution of the Grand Lodge of Louisiana of Free and Accepted Masons. Under the terms of the agreement of the merger, the Louisiana Grand Lodge members became recognized as "regular" by the Grand Lodge of Louisiana. All Lodges chartered by the Louisiana Grand Lodge (or by the Grand Lodge of Mississippi in Louisiana) passed under the jurisdiction of the new Grand Lodge of Louisiana. While the new constitution appeared to merge the two Grand Lodges, the Grand Lodge of Louisiana was, in effect, taken over by the Louisiana Grand Lodge. All non-York Rite Lodges were instructed to turn in their charters to receive new York Rite charters from the new Grand Lodge. Three Scottish Rite Lodges, *Etoile Polaire*, *Los Amigos del Orden*, and *Disciples of the Masonic Senate*, sought relief from the New Orleans Supreme Council. Of these events Foulhouze wrote:

> "It was agreed that the Grand Lodge should no more *cumulate* the rites, that it would have and keep its own forms, but that each Lodge in the East might freely work according to its particular and more favorite rite and tenets.
>
> Had that agreement been faithfully observed, another series of quiet days might have ensued in Louisiana: but the newcomers in the Grand Lodge soon showed that far from being sincere, they had crept into our bosom with the only view to tear it to pieces and to build their powers on the ruins of ours. [...]

They made as I had foreseen and foretold, a Constitution by which the Scotch lodges of the East were reduced to nought and the life members of the Grand Lodge expelled from it[38] the better to secure the triumph and power of those invaders.

But from the moment that the constitution began to work, the Scotch lodges understood their mistake; and not withstanding the blame thrown upon them by the new Grand Lodge which was as it was expected, did not fail to say that they were bound by the vote of the majority at Baton Rouge, they all parted from it, averting and showing that they had been deceived, and could not thus be fetted and annihilated by a paltry trick.

That event occasioned a good deal of rumor. The Mississippians who had snatched the power began promulgating their bulls of excom-munication. John Gedge, like his imitators of this present Consistory, wrote his reports, made his speeches, sent his circulars, but it was to no purpose.

The Supreme Council of Louisiana resumed its authority on the blue lodges of the Scotch rite, and the separation was con-summated.[39]

If the goal of the new 1850 Grand Lodge Constitution and the merger with the Louisiana Grand Lodge was to bring peace to all the Louisiana Masons, it was a total failure. If the goal was to remove the power base in the Grand Lodge from the French-speaking New Orleans Masons, it was, indeed, a success. The French-speaking New Orleans Masons became split after 1850. One faction, outraged at the turn of events, wished nothing more to do with the Grand Lodge and saw the Supreme Council as the only hope of maintaining the French interests. The other French faction, most likely very tired of the squabbles, remained with the Grand Lodge in the hopes of possibly still bringing unity to the troubled Grand Lodge.

The 1850 Union of the Grand Lodge resulted in a perceived need for action in the New Orleans Council. Foulhouze believed that he could strengthen the New Orleans Scottish Rite by expanding the number of 33rds in the Council. Foulhouze says of this:

> "Brother Canonge died and I was elected
> commander in his place. My first move was to promote
> to the 33d degree one or two members of each of the
> lodges then established and of some importance in the
> city of New Orleans, hoping that their initiation would
> be the best means to secure the masonic peace in our
> East, as it would contribute to carry light where it was
> most needed." [40]

During Foulhouze's administration of the Supreme Council of
Louisiana prior to the Concordat, he elevated approximately 30
Masons to the 33rd degree in the New Orleans Council. [41] Those
elevated to the 33rd degree by Foulhouze included Charles Claiborne,
Thomas Wharton Collens (22 June 1849), Claude Pierre Samory and
Charles Laffon de Ladébat (11 February 1852). The wisdom of
expanding the membership of the Supreme Council was apparently
recognized by Albert Pike on 25 March 1859 (Pike's first SC Session
as Grand Commander) when he expanded the Membership in the
Charleston Council from 9 Members to 33 Members.

Charles Claiborne assumed the post of Secretary General for the
New Orleans Council and T. Wharton Collens, that of Lt. Grand
Commander. The Foulhouze/Collens relationship was a very close
one which continued until Foulhouze's death in 1875 - years after
both had resigned from Masonry. Foulhouze and Collens would, in
the early 1850's, even share a law office.

The Lopez Expedition and James Foulhouze

If the Union of 1850 between the Grand Lodge of Louisiana and
the Louisiana Grand Lodge, along with the many bomb shells from
that event, were not enough to occupy the minds of the Louisiana
Masons, an event took place simultaneously that over-shadowed the
Masonic events in Louisiana and be thrust into the forefront of the
minds and thoughts of all Americans. This international event
directly played a part in future New Orleans Masonic "battles."

In 1849 Narciso Lopez, a Venezuelan and former colonel in the
Spanish Army, began a campaign to take control of Cuba and replace
the Spanish government on the island with his own government.
Lopez received limited support from various U.S. politicians, but was

unable to raise a suitable sized army for his mission. Lopez found better luck in New Orleans where he was able to raise an army of approximately 750 men, mainly veterans of the Mexican War, and sail out of New Orleans in April of 1850 with the goal of capturing the island. The mission was a complete failure. The U.S. troops were slaughtered and Lopez was eventually captured and executed. Reports quickly came to the U.S. and the newspapers of the day reported the "murder" of the U.S. troops along with the capture and execution of not only troops, but vacationing U.S. tourists who happened to be on the island. New Orleans was an obvious "hot spot" for the Lopez Expedition as, not only did the expedition leave from New Orleans, but the city contained many Spanish speaking citizens from Cuba. The Grand Lodge of Louisiana had also chartered two Lodges in Cuba during the early years of the Grand Lodge.[42] The tie between New Orleans and Cuba was close for both the general and Masonic population.

James Foulhouze became entwined in the Lopez Expedition when he traveled to Cuba at the height of the crisis. A New Orleans newspaper, the *Daily Delta*, ran a story on Foulhouze vehemently criticizing his trip, and suggesting that he was, possibly, a spy for the Spanish government.[43] The very evening following the publication of the article concerning Foulhouze, T. Wharton Collens and Robert Preaux published an article in the *Daily Picayune* explaining that Foulhouze's trip to Cuba was with the goal of, hopefully, securing the release of vacationing U.S. citizens who were caught in the conflict.[44] Foulhouze, being made a Mason in a Spanish speaking Lodge, had numerous interactions with New Orleans Masons from Cuba. In addition, Foulhouze had gained the confidence of various Spanish officials on the island of Cuba through acting as legal council for them several years earlier. Along with the article published by Collens and Preaux, the *Delta* article on Foulhouze received censure by a number of competing New Orleans newspapers. The *Delta* article was exposed to be a newspaper "thriller" story with little basis in fact. One newspaper entitling an article critical of the *Delta's* lack of support for its charges "Newspaper Intolerance"[45] and another paper calling a report on Foulhouze's trip "A Mission of Humanity."[46] The *Delta* ran one more article in defense of its position claiming that the matter would be settled when Foulhouze returned to New Orleans and the entire event would be brought to the attention of the public.[47]

Nothing more, however, was published on the matter by the *Delta*. The event passed from the public's attention and was attributed to one newspaper's attempt to sensationalize anything concerning a recent event with the possible goal of increasing its sale of newspapers.

Enter the Charleston Supreme Council

John Gedge, who in 1849 was the Grand Master of the irregular Louisiana Grand Lodge, was elected Grand Master of the Grand Lodge of Louisiana for the year 1851. On 27 March 1851 the New Orleans Council issued a manifesto in its own defense. This manifesto examined the New Orleans situation and was an appeal for the establishment of fraternal relations between the New Orleans Council and other Masonic Bodies world-wide. With Louisiana Masonry in a state of turmoil and the once powerful Supreme Council of Louisiana fighting for order and stability, the time for the Charleston Council to act was at hand.

At the invitation of John Gedge, Albert Mackey came to New Orleans in February of 1852 and established, for the Charleston Council, a Consistory of the 32°. Gedge served as Commander in Chief. The establishment of this Charleston Consistory in New Orleans resulted in a new wave of turmoil and paved the way for the Concordat of 1855 merging the Charleston and New Orleans Councils.

The Supreme Council of Louisiana responded to the Charleston Consistory in New Orleans by taking several measures. A notice critical of the new consistory was place in the *New Orleans Bee* by the Supreme Council of Louisiana on 27 February 1852.[48] The notice carried the names of the then 29 Active Members[49] of the New Orleans Council. The New Orleans Council, also, incorporated itself under the official name of "Supreme Council of the Thirty-three [sic] and last degree of the Ancient and Accepted Scotch Rite for the United States of America, sitting at New Orleans, State of Louisiana." The act of incorporation was signed on 7 June 1852 and approved by the Secretary of State, the noted Charles Gayarre, on 13 January 1853.[50]

In July of 1852 Foulhouze traveled to New York to install Henry C. Atwood as Grand Commander of the "Sup-reme Council of the Thirty-third Degree of and for the Free, Sovereign and Inde-pendent State of New York" and then journeyed on to France in an attempt to enlist French support for his cause. It is noteworthy that Foulhouze embraced the concept that Supreme Councils should be limited to state jurisdictions just as Grand Lodges.[51]

The Concordat of 1855

The speed in which the total loss of the Grand Lodge of Louisiana by the French-speaking Masons occurred caused obvious confusion and uncertainty as to the future. James Foulhouze, as Grand Commander of the New Orleans Supreme Council, sought to unite all of the French-speaking Masons under his banner. Whether it was because of the rapid advancement of Foulhouze (resulting in uncertainty in his ability) or simply personality conflicts, Foulhouze was unable to unite all of the French Masons. The conflict of opinions within the New Orleans Supreme Council as to the direction in which to proceed can reasonably be seen as a contributing factor to the resignation of Foulhouze on 30 July 1853 and nearly all of the officers of the New Orleans Council by December of 1853. The final break for Foulhouze appears to have occurred at the 22 June meeting of the New Orleans Council. At that meeting, T. Wharton Collens, the Lt. Grand Commander, had prepared a series of resolutions to present to the Council. After a reading of the resolutions, the floor was opened for comment, but instead of addressing the points of the various resolutions, Charles Claiborne apparently began a series of attacks on Foulhouze's clothing. The meeting fell into shouting matches and the deep rooted feelings of frustration from the events of the past years seemingly boiled up. Foulhouze, realizing that control of the meeting was lost, closed the Council and departed.[52]

In the absence of the Minutes of the New Orleans Council during the Foulhouze years[53] it can only be presumed that T. Wharton Collens assumed the post of acting Grand Commander for the remainder of 1853 until his own resignation on 19 December of that year. The day following the resignation of Collens, the Grand Treasurer, Jean Baptiste Faget, turned in his letter of resignation and an undated letter of resignation from the Grand Secretary, J.J.E. Massicott, was also accepted by the Council.

On 7 January 1854, Charles Claiborne was elected Grand Commander of the New Orleans Council. Claude Pierre Samory was elected Lt. Grand Commander and Charles Laffon de Ladébat was appointed Grand Secretary. Samory and Ladébat were part of the

French-speaking faction that split from Foulhouze during the 1850-53 turmoil. 1854 was devoted to negotiations with the Charleston Supreme Council. 6 & 17 February 1855 the concordat merging the New Orleans and Charleston Supreme Councils was signed. Present in New Orleans for the signing of the Concordat, and representing the Charleston Council, were Albert Mackey and John Quitman. John Gedge, who had spearheaded the movement of the Louisiana Grand Lodge and the 1852 Consistory, did not live to see the concordat between the New Orleans and Charleston Councils - he died on 13 April 1854 during a yellow fever epidemic in New Orleans.

The death of Gedge must have created some concern for the future of the newly reorganized Scottish Rite Masonry in New Orleans. Gedge had led a complete and total coup of the Grand Lodge, dramatically altering its nature. It was, also, Gedge who had written to Mackey to bring a Charleston consistory to New Orleans and took control of this consistory as he did the Grand Lodge. The introduction of the Charleston consistory paved the way for the Concordat of 1855. His influence on the events of the times is unquestionable. It is reasonable to assume that Gedge might have taken some position of leadership in the post concordat days - had he lived. It is logical that Gedge would have become an Active Member of the Charleston Supreme Council and led the reorganized Grand Consistory of Louisiana. The death of Gedge made this impossible, yet the basic problem remained. A powerful figure was needed to lead and unite the very fragmented New Orleans Scottish Rite. Regardless of the fact that the concordat had taken place, there were still quite a number of former New Orleans Council 33rds unaffiliated with the Charleston Council - or any Council. The potential for uprising was undeniable. In a letter to Claude Samory, Albert Mackey suggested that the man to lead and unite the New Orleans Scottish Rite Masons had been found and it was believed that only the formalities remained. Mackey wrote:

> I hope to be present at the installation of that Bro:. as S:.G:.I:.G:. whose adhesion to us will heal all difficulties [...] The moment we receive your nomination, the nominated Bro:. will be elected.[54]

The man Mackey wrote of was James Foulhouze. The choosing of Foulhouze to join the Charleston Council and lead the New Orleans Scottish Rite *for* the Charleston Council is very reasonable and, given the situation, the only logical choice that could be made. Foulhouze was viewed as a regular 33rd from the Grand Orient of France. As Foulhouze was also a former Grand Commander of the New Orleans Supreme Council who had resigned prior to the concordat, he might have been viewed as something of a prominent "free agent." The fact that Foulhouze was a member (and even Grand Commander) of the New Orleans Council was irrelevant from a regularity stand point. If he agreed to join with the Charleston Council then this matter could be easily settled. Samory and Ladébat were also members of the New Orleans Council (and both given the 33rd degree *by* Foulhouze) yet both became Active Members and officers of the Charleston Council. If James Foulhouze agreed to lead the New Orleans Scottish Rite, under the Charleston Council banner, the Charleston Council would have a much easier road to travel in bringing the remainder of the New Orleans Scottish Rite Masons under their control. Foulhouze was approached by Albert Mackey and Claude Samory in the summer of 1856 and offered the position of Commander-in-Chief of the Grand Consistory and Active Membership in the Southern Jurisdiction providing that he joined the Charleston camp.[55] Of this event Foulhouze wrote:

> About a year or fifteen months ago, M. Antonio Costa asked me whether I had any objection to converse with M. Claude Samory about the then state of affairs with regard to the Scottish Rite in Louisiana. I answered that I had none. On the following day M. Samory together with M. Costa called on me, and in his presence, told me that he had long been anxious to see me, that he was always my friend, that the course which he and other members of the Supreme Council of Louisiana had followed since I left it was with the only view of putting an end to any further contest and quarrel both with the Grand Lodge of our state and the Supreme Council of Charleston, that many a York mason of this east was now initiated to the high degrees of the Scottish Rite, that they all had heard of me as

being well versed in its tenets and ceremonies, and were anxious to see me join the Consistory thereto assume the command of the Rite in Louisiana, that indeed I had just cause to complain of the conduct of some BB:. towards me both in the Supreme Council and in the Polar Star Lodge, but that they all acknowledged it, and were ready on my joining the Grand Consistory, to offer me any apology I might wish, that there was a vacancy in the Supreme Council of Charleston which he had been offered to fill, and which he was ready to give up in my behalf if I would unite with them, that my presence in that Council would do immense good both here and at Charleston, and that the best I could do was to accept, if I desired to carry out my opinion and views with regard to the right which Louisiana has to its Supreme Council.

My answer to M. Samory was as follows:

I need no apology, for any thing which may have been done or said in any masonic body to hurt my feelings. Masonry, thank God, has taught me better desires, and it is enough for me to hear from you that all those who may have had an intention to offend me, do now regret it. As to your proposal, I can in no way or manner accept it. My position is clear and well defined. The Supreme Council of Louisiana was not founded by me. It existed before I was a mason. In 1845 I received, not in the Supreme Council of France founded by M. Grasse de Tilly, but in the Supreme Council of the Grand Orient, the 33d degree. That most Illustrious body treated me as a future member of the Supreme Council of Louisiana with which it corresponded, and I was commissioned by its Grand Commander and other members to be the interpreter of their good feelings near our Supreme Council. A short time after my return here, our Grand Commander Jean François Canonge died, and I was elected to replace him. On doing so, I bound myself to obey it and protect its rights: and I must say that after a most serious inquiry into its origin and the sources from which it emanates, I am more than ever convinced that my opinion with regard to the fundamental authority of the Scottish Rite is correct, and that the views of Charleston thereon are altogether erroneous. From the moment you and other 33rds of this East judged fit to recognize the Council of Charleston as your superior, I and two other members of our Supreme Council, did immediately exercise what, in such case we considered to be our right, and continued the work of our Supreme Council. It is true that on account of the momentary excitement which has prevailed, we have chosen to be silent, but we exist nevertheless and have resolved to safeguard our power and authority for any case of emergency. I certainly feel much honored with the proposition which you make me to accept an appointment as an active member of the Supreme Council of Charleston and as such to preside your Consistory here, but neither such a flattering offer, nor any other consideration can make me deviate from what I consider to be my duty towards a body which I have sworn to protect. I have personally no pretension whatsoever to power. I know that I am good only to make an initiation, and I acknowledge that the privilege of commanding should be better placed in other hands than mine. Many a person, no doubt, will attribute my determination to a spirit of opposition, but as I feel good will towards all and even those who condemn me both in York and Scotish [sic] ranks of Masonry, I will, happen what it may, persevere following the line which I believe to be the only correct one.

Thereupon, M. Samory expressed his hope that I would change my mind, and asked me whether I would like to converse with M. Albert G. Mackey on that subject. I answered affirmatively and two or three days afterward, he called at my house with that Gentleman.

M. Mackey began by expressing a desire that his visit to me should not be considered as official. I replied that being both knights templars, we were authorized to meet as such and talk of the questions relative to the Scotish Rite, as if we were perfect strangers to it; and it being so agreed, he repeated to me all that M. Samory had said before with regard to the desire expressed by a large number of masons that I should join the consistory, and with regard to my being made an active member of the Council of Charleston and taking as such command of the Scotish rite in Louisiana. I answered him what I had already answered M. Samory. A few words where then exchanged between him and me, with regard to the origin of the council of Charleston, the constitutions of 1786, the authority which the Supreme Council of the Grand Orient of France claims on the Scotish degrees and the differences which exists between the York and Scotish rites. He admitted that difference and that the reasons which I gave upon all the other points presented a strong matter of consideration, but that he could not accept them as conclusive, which I immediately understood and acknowledged to be with him a matter of course.

He then insisted that I should again consider the proposition made by Mr. C. Samory, and confirmed by himself; and in conclusion he wished me to let him know what my determination would be after more mature reflection.

I promised to do so through Mr. Samory: and this Gentleman having called on me some weeks afterwards, and repeated all that he had been kind enough to say at his first interview with me, I again answered that I could not accept: and I remember having thus addressed him in the end:

'My dear Sir, in the same manner as the masons whom you now represent, express a desire to have me in your Consistory for their best interest, so a time may come when Scotish masons of this East, tired of a

foreign dominion, shall be glad to know that there is
in New Orleans a 33d of some value who has never
varied, and can at any time be the strong hold around
which they may gather as Louisianians.'

Thereon we parted good friends as I parted with
Mr. Mackey, after due interchange of kindness and
politeness. [56]

In 1858, Charles Laffon de Ladébat, while clearly bitter towards
Foulhouze, commented on this meeting between Foulhouze, Samory
and Mackey:

Ill Bros. Mackey and Samory knew very well that with
a few persons, amoung the weak minded and the
ignorant, Mr. Foulhouze was "somebody," and that if
they could prevail on him to join the Grand Consistory
of Louisiana, peace would be finally restored, and it
was solely for the purpose of securing that peace, that
they paid him a visit, against the advise of many who
knew Mr. Foulhouze better than they. [57]

With John Gedge dead and Foulhouze no longer in consideration, Claude Samory became the first New Orleans Mason to be
elected an Active member of the Charleston Council. His election
was on 20 November 1856. On 17 December 1856, the Grand
Consistory filled the vacancy offered to James Foulhouze. The choice
was a Mason of promise but of little training in the Scottish Rite. The
attorney from Arkansas, Albert Pike, was unanimously (and in his
absence [58]) elected Commander in Chief of the Grand Consistory of
Louisiana.

Prior to the election of Samory and Pike, Foulhouze took part in
an activity which sealed his fate with the Charleston Council. James
Foulhouze, along with T.W. Collens, J.J.E. Massicott, J.B. Faget and
other former members of the Supreme Council of Louisiana declared,
in effect, the Concordat of 1855 invalid and publicly resumed the
activities of the New Orleans Council. The date that the New Orleans
Council was re-opened is sometimes disputed. Foulhouze stated in
November of 1857:

> From the moment I had noticed of that nameless act [the Concordat of 1855], I called upon some 33ds, whom I knew to be true to their obligations, and with them I immediately opened the Supreme Council and continued its work, in order that it might not even be said that it had slept a single instant ...[59]

If such a meeting of 33rds did take place, it was still not until 9 October 1856 that J.J.E. Massicott would be elected Grand Commander of the reorganized Supreme Council of Louisiana and their activities become public. That action was the "shot" which started a new round of Masonic turbulence which dramatically altered the nature of the U.S. Scottish Rite.

The re-origination of the Supreme Council of Louisiana

The days/months/years following the concordat were a time of great uncertainty with many New Orleans Masons. The arguments made by all sides sounded somewhat reasonable. An examination of who chose to associate with the Charleston Council after the concordat, who choose to associate with the revived New Orleans Council and who chose to associate with neither body provides an interesting look into the divided, confused and emotional state of affairs. Of the Grand Lodge of Louisiana officers who were Active Members of the New Orleans Council in the pre-concordat days, two of the five Past Grand Masters[60] chose to affiliate with neither body. One affiliated with the Charleston Council[61] and two with the revived New Orleans Council.[62] Of the eight senior Grand Lodge officers, two chose to affiliate with neither body,[63] two with the Charleston Council[64] and four with the revived New Orleans Council.[65] Of the non- Grand Lodge New Orleans 33rds in the pre-concordat days, 8 chose to associate with neither body, 15 with the Charleston Council and 4 with the revived New Orleans Council. The totals then would be: 12 choosing to affiliate with neither body, 19 with the Charleston Council and 10 with the revived New Orleans Council. These figures should not, however, be viewed as the final tally as they were, over the following years, modified as members moved from one body to the other in a most disconcerting manner. L. E. Deluzain, who was a participant in the 1855 Concordat affiliating with the Charleston

Council, re-affiliated with the revived New Orleans Council upon its revival. Joseph Lamarre, who was created a 33rd in the revived New Orleans Council on 25 February 1858, was tried and expelled by that Council on 22 May 1858. He then affiliated with the Grand Consistory of Louisiana becoming an Honorary 33rd. Neither side could truly claim clear victory as the severely bitter strife left both sides with ragged edges. Many of those who chose one side or the other eventually retired from any Masonic affiliation.

Possibly concerned over the reorganization of the New Orleans Council, the Grand Consistory of Louisiana sought to organize itself into a state corporation in early 1857. On 19 March 1857 the General Assembly of the Louisiana State Senate and House of Representatives approved the incorporation of the Grand Consistory of Louisiana. Listed as members were two future Sovereign Grand Commanders of the Charleston Council - Albert Pike and James C. Batchelor. On 22 April 1857 Foulhouze was elected Grand Commander of the revived New Orleans Council. T. Wharton Collens resumed his former position as Lt. Grand Commander. With Foulhouze back in command, the New Orleans Council began to grow in strength and size. 1858 was a pivotal year for Foulhouze and the reorganized New Orleans Supreme Council. In February, Albert Pike delivered a lecture before the Grand Lodge of Louisiana. His lecture was a sharp assault on Foulhouze and the New Orleans Council. The lecture by Pike, and arguments against it, occupied most of the March 1858 issue of the *Masonic Delta*.[66] Clearly the Charleston camp had found a Mason as capable of the "stinging pen" as Foulhouze. February 1858 also brought a commanding new (returning) member to the New Orleans Council. The announcement in the *Masonic Delta* was sure to cause great concern in the Charleston/New Orleans camp:

> We are happy to say that our most Ill:. and worthy Bro:. Pierre Soulé has joined the Supreme Council of the 33d, in and for the Sovereign and Independent State of Louisiana. This eminent citizen and learned Freemason admits thus the State Rights masonically as well as politically.[67]

The return of this fiery and powerful former United States Senator and U.S. Minister to Spain to the rolls of the New Orleans Supreme

Council was the equivalent of a shot of adrenaline for the New Orleans Council. Soulé was created a 33rd on 8 March 1838 by Jean Jacques Conte and was, actually, a Member of the New Orleans Supreme Council prior to the election of Foulhouze as Grand Com-mander. Soulé apparently resigned from the Council at some point following Foulhouze's election as his name is no where to be found in any of the records concerning the Concordat of 1855. There are no known record giving the reasons for the resignation of Soulé from the Council nor his Masonic activities during, or thoughts of, the concordat. Soulé was elected a U.S. Senator in 1847 and served in that office until 1853 followed by his appointment as Minister to Spain from 1853-55. Soulé was a vocal, resourceful and respected addition to the New Orleans Council.

The addition of Pierre Soulé as an Active Member of the New Orleans Council would seem to be answered one month later by the addition of Albert Pike as an Active Member of the Charleston Council on 20 March 1858. [68] At the very session which elected Pike as an Active Member, Foulhouze was formally "expelled" from the Scottish Rite by the Charleston Council. Since Foulhouze was never a member of any Body controlled by the Charleston Council, this action was more of a public statement of disapproval than an actual expulsion. What followed next was a series of "sledge hammer" verbal and written attacks from and upon both the New Orleans and Charleston Councils. The extremely bitter attacks surpassed even the Cerneau "war" which resulted in the death of all "High Grade" Scottish Rite Masonry in the U.S. with the exception of in New Orleans. Foulhouze released his *Mémoire à Consulter* in French in 1858 and, then in 1859, issue his *Historical Inquiry into the Origin of the Ancient and Accepted Scottish Rite* in English. [69] The book served as the platform from which Foulhouze stated his case, defined his actions and views on regularity as well as his concepts of the history of the Scottish Rite. Foulhouze also used the *Masonic Delta* as a platform. This monthly publication was he official organ of the revived Supreme Council of Louisiana. Joseph Lamarre released his *A Masonic Trial in New Orleans* in French in 1858 and Charles Laffon de Ladébat translated and added notes to the work for an English edition. The next major New Orleans Masonic publication was a work designed to answer Foulhouze's *Mémoire à Consulter* and further state the position of the Charleston Supreme Council. *A Dissection of the Manifesto of Mr. Charles Bienvenu* was released 1858 and opened a very regrettable door for the Charleston Council. The work, while originally issued as an anonymous publication, was later learned to be the work of Albert Pike and Charles Laffon de Ladébat. While the *Dissection* was as harsh in tone as Foulhouze's *Mémoire à Consulter*, it went back to the Lopez Expedition period and re-printed in the end of the booklet the article published on Foulhouze by the *Daily Delta* and the retort by T. Wharton Collens and Robert Preaux. What was not published, nor mentioned, was the response of nearly all of the competing New Orleans newspapers condemning the yellow journalistic style of the *Delta's* article on Foulhouze. The illusion created in the *Dissection* was that the *Delta's* article on Foulhouze was factual and Collens and Preaux were only attempting to deny the obvious. In 1873, James Scot published his *Outline of the Rise and Progress of Freemasonry in Louisiana* and reveal that the *Dissection* influenced his thinking and beliefs (and assuredly that of many others) of Foulhouze. Scot says of Foulhouze:

> At this time [1850] he [Foulhouze] was charged with being a spy of the Spanish Government, and was afterwards denounced as such in the newspapers of the day when the news of the fate of the Lopez expedition reached New Orleans. During the excitement he was concealed by some friends to prevent his falling into the hands of the mob, until he was able to effect his escape to Havana. He afterward returned, and resigned his membership in the Supreme Council, July 30, 1853. [70]

James Foulhouze was not viewed as one who simply held a very strong opposing Masonic opinion and followed a course of action that he felt was correct, he was now portrayed as a charlatan of low moral character. This was quite a different picture than the Mason who was approached by Albert Mackey to become an Active Member of the Charleston Supreme Council. The statement by Scot is erroneous. The only newspaper which published such a opinion of Foulhouze was denounced by the balance of the newspapers in New Orleans. Foulhouze went to Havana in an attempt to secure the release of American citizens *prior* to the article by the *Delta*. He did not "escape" to Havana. The Scot quotation is an example of the emotional and confused state of affairs in Louisiana Masonry and the fact that inaccuracies were, sadly, sometimes accept as fact.

On 3 October 1858 Foulhouze informed the New Orleans Council, in Session, of a communication he received from the Grand Orient of France. Foulhouze, as a Grand Orient 33rd, was officially instructed to disassociate himself from the revived New Orleans Council. Foulhouze refused this mandate. On 4 February 1859 the Grand Orient of France struck Foulhouze's name from its list of 33rds.

Despite the actions taken and the decrees and publications written against Foulhouze and the New Orleans Council, there was no sign that the Council was weakening. In fact, the New Orleans Council showed every indication of strengthening. By 1859 the Supreme Council of Louisiana was at its peak of power in the post concordat days. Twenty-five active lodges were under its jurisdiction[71] and the Council was composed of thirty-four Active Members.[72] Of the lodges under the jurisdiction of the New Orleans Council, seven were located outside of New Orleans in various regions of Louisiana. The make-up of the lodges reveal that the popularity of the New Orleans Council was not solely with the French speaking New Orleans Masons. Twelve lodges worked in the French language, seven in the English language, two in German, one in Italian and one in Spanish. Remembering the fact that the Louisiana Grand Lodge (with its "irregular" stamp) grew in power and took over the Grand Lodge of Louisiana in 1850 with no outside support, save the Grand Lodge of Mississippi, the matter of the New Orleans Council had to be addressed. It was not simply a growing threat to the Charleston Council, but, also, to the Grand Lodge of Louisiana.

With no real structure, rituals or organization, the Charleston Council apparently began to realize that it was, indeed, in trouble. Of this time Charles S. Lobingier, 33°, G.C. writes in his 1931 *The Supreme Council, 33°:*

> Both Pike and Mackey had by this time decided that the Supreme Council needed reform. On January 20, 1858, the former had written the latter urging an increase in the membership and the introduction of the elective system.[73]

For reasons that are, at best, ambiguous, Grand Commander John Honour resigned his office in the Charleston Council on 13 August 1858. It was not until 2 January 1859 that Albert Pike was proclaimed, by Albert Mackey, *elected* to the office of Grand Commander of the Charleston Supreme Council. It is logical that the actions of Foulhouze and the New Orleans Council influenced the change of command in the Charleston Council. Pike immediately began to reform the Charleston Council and make the changes necessary for its survival. In 1860 Foulhouze was elected to the judgeship of the Second District Court in Plaquemines Parish. In 1861 Foulhouze moved his domicile from New Orleans to Plaquemines Parish. That same year former judge and Lt. Grand Commander T. Wharton Collens was elected Judge of the Seventh District Court in New Orleans. On 2 January 1861 the New Orleans Council re-incorporated itself taking officially, for the first time, the name "The Supreme Council of Louisiana." Due to the pressures of his new position, T.W. Collens resigned in 1861 as Lt. Grand Commander of the New Orleans Council. He was replaced by Sam Brown, who was created a 33rd by Foulhouze 5 March 1860.

The Civil War

Arguably there has been no lower point in the history of the United States then the Civil War years of 1861-65. The divided country nearly destroyed itself in four years of devastating war, the effects of which plagued the county for a century to follow. While there has been numerous accounts of Masonic acts of charity during the war years, the war weakened Masonry in the U.S. due to the loss of life, property and the economic hardship that followed the war years. There is no sign or record that any of the Supreme Councils in the U.S. were active during the Civil Wars years. Pierre Soulé was imprisoned for a time upon the capture of New Orleans in 1862. Upon his release from prison, he lived out the remaining war years in Cuba. Albert Pike was charged with war crimes stemming from the Battle at Pea Ridge (his only war command) and was left out of the general amnesty afforded at the close of the war. Pike fled to Canada awaiting a Presidential pardon allowing him to return to the U.S. There are no known records of the Supreme Council of Louisiana during the war years and it is unknown what events, if any, took place in the Council during this time. James Foulhouze, who prior to the war was a district court judge is shown to be a Parish Attorney for Plaquemines Parish following the war. There are no records of the exact date that he left office as a judge, nor giving the reasons. It is possible that the then 65 year old Foulhouze simply retired from his judgeship or his leaving office might have been required by the Union in the post war years. A series of events that can best be described as "amazing" then takes place concerning Foulhouze and the New Orleans Council.

On 3 May 1866, T. Wharton Collens, Pierre Soulé and 8 other 33rds of the New Orleans Council signed an "oath of allegiance" to the New Orleans Council.[74] Foulhouze's name is not included in this apparent reorganization. On 10 May 1866, the New Orleans Council obtained the oath of allegiance of Robert Preaux and created two 33rds. One of the 33rds created was a New Orleans music teacher, music shop owner and composer of moderate note who corresponded with many of the artistic and literary figures in Europe including Victor Hugo. His name was Eugene Chassaignac. On 7 January 1867, Chassaignac was elected Grand Commander of the Supreme Council of Louisiana. It is unknown who was Grand Commander or "acting" Grand Commander at the time that Chassaignac was elevated to the 33d degree or why Chassaignac was selected to lead the New Orleans Council. There is a total veil of mystery over the election of Chassaignac and the departure of Foulhouze.

The 1 May 1867 minutes of *Liberty* Lodge #19 (under the New Orleans Council's jurisdiction)[75] show that O.J Dunn, Grand Master of the Eureka Grand Lodge of Louisiana (Prince Hall) and five other Prince Hall Lodges in various locations in the U.S. had officially accepted the invitation to attend *Liberty* Lodge and noted that this Lodge admitted visitors with no regard to race. The Worshipful Master of *Liberty* Lodge was Eugene Chassaignac. The New Orleans Council, likewise and that same year, officially announced that membership to its lodges were not be based on race. That announcement, in itself, seems curious as the Supreme Council of Louisiana (and the whole of New Orleans Masonry) had a long history, prior to the Civil War, of having little concern over race and Masonic membership.

In an amazing and dramatic move, the Grand Orient of France, ignoring its past action against James Foulhouze, re-recognized the Supreme Council of Louisiana on 5 November 1868. Eugene

Chassaignac commented on James Foulhouze and the relations with the Grand Orient of France in the April-May 1869 issue of the *Bulletin:*
[76]

> It is true that in 1858, following the writings of Mr. J. Foulhouze, (writings that were not at all the acts of the Supreme Council) our relations with the Grand Orient were interrupted; but since I have had the honor of being the Grand Commander and Grand Master of the Scotch Rite, in Louisiana, I had the pamphlets disavowed by a solemn resolution; on the other hand, Mr. Foulhouze not being any longer a member of our order, there no longer exists a reason for the relations between the Grand Orient of France and the Supreme Council of Louisiana to be interrupted.[77]

What happened? Without James Foulhouze the reorganization of the New Orleans Council would have failed before it started. The Chassaignac statement can only be viewed as incredible and shows an almost contempt for Foulhouze. Why? There is no clue as to what could have taken place during the Civil War years. Prior to the war the New Orleans Council was at its height of power and could have in a matter of a few years, realistically, overpowered the Charleston Council and seriously threatened the Grand Lodge of Louisiana had the war not interrupted its growth. James Foulhouze was the power and the driving force of this movement. It simply could not have happened without him. There is not a hint as to why Foulhouze left office, why Chassaignac was made a 33rd, why Chassaignac was elected Grand Commander or why Chassaignac seemingly turned on Foulhouze. Just as perplexing as the Chassaignac statement on Foulhouze is the re-recognition of the New Orleans Council by the Grand Orient. The Grand Orient had stripped Foulhouze of his 33rd Degree for his participation in the reorganization of the New Orleans Council. Why would they now recognize that very same Body? The re-recognition of the New Orleans Council by the Grand Orient of France unquestionably caused great concern in the Supreme Councils SJ and NMJ. In a bold move, relations between the Grand Orient and the SJ and NMJ were suspended by a join resolution of the SJ and NMJ dated 2 May and 15 June 1870. The resolution made the following points (presumably written by Pike).

"The Grand Orient of France well knew, for it had so decided in a sane interval, in 1858, that an Inspector-General created by itself could exercise no powers within the jurisdiction of another Supreme Council. It knew that the Chassaignac body was created by the sole authority of M. Jacques Foulhouze, whom it had denuded of his privileges as an Inspector-General, for *"forfaiture d'honneur,"* in establishing it. And yet, without any new light upon the subject, without any reconsideration or reexamination, without restoring M. Foulhouze, and while in alliance with us, it recognized this spurious organization as a lawful Supreme Council." [78]

The Death of James Foulhouze

There is no suggestion that Foulhouze had any connection with Masonry following the Civil War years. In 1869 Foulhouze co-authored a book with William M. Prescott titled *The Ordinances of the Police Jury of the Parish of Plaquemines.* Foulhouze is listed as "Parish Attorney" and Prescott as "Parish Judge." Foulhouze apparently busied himself with legal matters and spent the remainder of his life in the Mississippi River town of Pointe-a-la-Hache, Louisiana.

On 21 December 1875 the following article appeared in the *New Orleans Bee*:

> "Deceased the 18th of December 1875 at Pointe-a-la Hache, parish of Plaquemines, the Hon. James Foulhouze at the age of seventy-five. A native of Riom, Auvergue, France."

Foulhouze was buried at St. Thomas the Apostle Church Cemetery in Pointe-a-la-Hache, Louisiana. T. Wharton Collens, who had by then also resigned from all Masonic activities, handled the legal matters concerning Foulhouze's succession. Collens wrote of Foulhouze:

> "I was very intimately acquainted with the late James Foulhouze during the thirty years that preceded his death. He was a native of Riom in France, and during the thirty years that I knew him he frequently

spoke to me of his relatives in that country, and showed me his correspondences with them. His father died previous to 1830, his mother a few years before he 'J. Foulhouze' did. He had a brother who died before he did - that brother left one heir a daughter. Foulhouze himself was never married." [79]

While Foulhouze not, by any means, a man of great wealth, he did own a home in Pointe-a-la-Hache and some property. Foulhouze's entire estate was willed to Odéalie Collens McCaleb, the married daughter of his long time friend T. Wharton Collens and Odéalie's son, James Foulhouze McCaleb.

The many unanswered questions concerning Foulhouze, and the events surrounding him may never be fully answered or understood. It is clear, however, that James Foulhouze followed a path which he honestly felt to be correct. Regardless of which side of the issue one takes, it must be objectively recognized that the impact that Foulhouze had on the whole of U.S. Scottish Rite Masonry was substantial. It must, also, be pointed out that those who supported and held the same opinion as Foulhouze were neither "weak minded" nor "ignorant" as sometimes charged. Differing opinions are frequently held by intelligent people. It is unfortunate when judgment is colored by emotion and it is tragic when erroneous conclusions born of skewed judgment makes its way into accepted history.

Notes:

1. *The Masonic Delta* March 1858.
2. This date was obtained from the tombstone of James Foulhouze located in St. Thomas the Apostle Church Cemetery, Pointe a la Hache, Louisiana.
3. Personal letter: Christine McCullough, Assistant Archivist, Archdiocese of Philadelphia to Michael R. Poll, 23 April 1993.
4. *Passenger and Immigration List Index Vol. I* P. William Filby, Mary K. Meyer Editors. (Detroit, Michigan: Gale Research Co., 1981) 314.
5. Charles Laffon de Ladébat, translator, notes of *A Masonic Trial in New Orleans* . (New Orleans, LA: J. Lamarre, 1858) p. 62.
6. *Encyclopedia Britannica Vol. XI* (Chicago: William Benton, Publisher, 1965) 814.
7. McCullough to Poll, 23 April 1993. It should be noted that a priest having his faculties suspended is akin to a physician having his medical license suspended. The affected priest would no longer be able to carry out the

duties of a priest such as hearing confessions, preforming wedding, baptisims, Mass, etc. While a priest who has had his faculties suspended is, in fact, prevented from doing all that makes one a priest, it is only the Vatican who can separate a priest from his vows as a priest. This would mean that Foulhouze might have, technically, remained a priest, without powers, until his death.

8. At the time that Foulhouze was a priest, Philadelphia was a "Diocese" and not yet an "Archdiocese."

9. McCullough to Poll, 23 April 1993.

10. Ladébat, notes, *A Masonic Trial in New Orleans* p. 62.

11. Philadelphia : U. Hunt, 1842.

12. The paper which Bishop Kenrick mentions was *Le Penseur* (The Thinker).

13. *Records of the American Catholic Historical Society Vol. VIII*, 1896 Bishop Kenrick to Dr. Cullen 23 November, 1843. 311-312.

14. Masonic and anti-Masonic

15. *The Louisiana Historical Quarterly Vol. 31, No. 4 October, 1948*. New Orleans, LA 918.

16. Roman Catholic law forbid duels regardless of the fact that, for many years, the traditional site for duels was in the gardens directly behind, and on the grounds of, the St. Louis Cathedral.

17. *The Masonic Delta* November 1857 edition.

18. Ibid.

19. Ibid.

20. James Foulhouze, *Historical Inquiry into the Origin of the Ancient and Accepted Scottish Rite* (New Orleans: True Delta Job Office, 1859.) 17.

21. *Masonic Delta* November 1857.

22. Canonge served the Grand Lodge of Louisiana as Grand Master in 1822-24 & 1829 and, also, served as Commander in Chief of the Grand Consistory of Louisiana from 1843-46. Canonge had served as the Grand Senior Warden of the Cerneau Grand Council of Princes of the Royal Secret, 32° in Philadelphia in 1818 and was an early member of the Supreme Council of Louisiana, being appointed Grand Expert on 7 November 1839. It was during Canonge's administration as Commander in Chief of the Grand Consistory that this body passed under the jurisdiction of the Supreme Council of Louisiana. Prior to his election to the office of Sovereign Grand Commander, Canonge served as the Lt. Grand Commander of the Supreme Council. Canonge had the reputation of being a "no nonsense" and "ready to act" individual with an amazing memory. As a criminal court judge he once ordered the arrest of the entire state Supreme Court for interfering in one of his capital trials. *New Orleans Times Democrat* 8 January 1893 "Louisiana Families"

23. *Masonic Delta* November 1857.

24. Foulhouze, *Historical Inquiry* p. 62.

25. See: *The Elimination of the French Influence in Louisiana Masonry* (New Orleans, LA: Michael Poll Publishing, 1996).

26. *Report of the Committee on Foreign Correspondence of the Louisiana Grand Lodge of Ancient York Masons.* (New Orleans: Cook, Young & Co., 1849.) 5.

27 Ibid. 5.

28. The town of Lafayette was a suburb of New Orleans in the 1800's located in what is now considered the "uptown" area of New Orleans.

29. George Washington, Lafayette, Warren, Marion, Crescent City, Hiram & Eureka.

30. *Grand Lodge of the State of Louisiana Report and Exposition* (New Orleans: J.L Sollée, 1849) 5-34.

31. James B. Scot, *Outline of the Rise and Progress of Freemasonry in Louisiana* 1873 (New Orleans, LA: Cornerstone Book Publishers, reprint 2008) 76.

32. Charles Laffon de Ladébat, *Ancient and Accepted Rite. Thirtieth Degree.* (New Orleans: 1857). xxvii.

33. Ladébat states in a footnote of his published 18° ritual: "The philosophical explanation of this and of all the other Degrees from the First up to the Thirtieth inclusive, is taken from the work of Ill.: Bro.: J. Foulhouze, 33d, with some slight alterations, of which, the author willingly assumes the responsibility." Ladébat, *Ancient and Accepted Scotch Rite. Eighteenth Degree* (New Orleans: 1856) 123. Foulhouze had, also, rewritten the 33° for the New Orleans Council. See: James D. Carter *History of the Supreme Council, 33° SJUSA (1861-1891).* (Washington, D.C.: The Supreme Council 33°, 1967). 37.

34. The title of this magazine is sometimes given as *Freemasons' Magazine.*

35. Charles S. Lobingier, *The Supreme Council , 33°* (Louisville, KY: The Standard Printing Co., Inc., 1931). 172; Ray Baker Harris, James D. Carter, *History of the Supreme Council, 33° SJUSA (1801-1861),* (Washington, DC: The Supreme Council 33°, 1964.) 236.

36. Minutes Book, Friends of Harmony Lodge #58 14 September 1849.

37. James Scot, *Outline of the Rise and Progress of Freemasonry in Louisiana.* New Orleans, LA: Cornerstone Book Publishers, reprint 2008. 78-80.

38. Prior to the Grand Lodge Constitution of 1850 Past Masters of the constituted lodges were made Life Members of the Grand Lodge with voting rights in the Grand Lodge. Following the Constitution of 1850, voting rights were only given to Grand Lodges Officers, the three principal members of each lodge, Past Grand Masters and Grand Lodge Committee members.

39. *The Masonic Delta* November 1857.

40. *The Masonic Delta* November 1857.

41. The numbers vary according to the source. *The Annual Grand Communication of the Supreme Council,* 1859, VIII lists 26 new 33rds. Albert Pike, *Official Bulletin VIII,* 1886 page 571-572 lists 31 new 33rds.

42. *Reunion Fraternal de Caridad* in Havana 12 July 1815 and *El Templo de la Devina Pastora* in Matanzaz 12 July 1818, *Proceedings of the Grand Lodge of Louisiana* 1995 (A-2 & 3).

43. *New Orleans Daily Delta* 31 May 1850.

44. *The Daily Picayune,* New Orleans, Louisiana 31 May 1850.

45. *The Daily Crescent* New Orleans, Louisiana 1 June 1850.

46. *Daily Orleanian,* New Orleans, Louisiana 2 June 1850.

47. *New Orleans Daily Delta* 1 June 1850.

48. *New Orleans Bee* 27 February 1852.

49. James Foulhouze, T.W. Collens, Charles Claiborne, J.B. Faget, Felix Garcia, F.A. Lumsden, Joseph Walker, John L. Lewis, Robert Preaux, Charles Murian, S. Heriman, Jean Lamothe, Antonio Costa, A. P. Lanaux, G.A. Montmain, F. Correjolles, J.H. Holland, R.D. Fanis, J.E. Jolly, J. Bachino, Aug. Broué, M. Prados, F. Ricau, J.J.E. Massicott, François Meilleur, C.M. Emerson, H.G. Duvivier, C. Samory & Charles Laffon.

50. *The Masonic Delta* August 1857.

51. An interesting document resides in the New Orleans Scottish Rite Library and Museum. It is a handwritten copy of the 1846 General Regulations of the New Orleans Supreme Council. This document is of special interest as it was used as a "working copy" for the 1848 General Regulations which were approved on 20 July 1848. The document contains the notes and changes throughout made by James Foulhouze with his signature. Clearly the various changes were presented to the Council for approval. The official name "The Supreme Council for the United States of America Sitting in New Orleans " at the head of the Regulations has portions scratched out leaving the only "The Supreme Council sitting in New Orleans." In addition, the side margins contain the proposed changes. In addition to the official name being altered to remove "for the United States of America" the proposed change to "for the State of Louisiana" written in the margin was also scratched out. Presumably the new title did not pass the vote of the Council or Foulhouze decided not to propose this name change - at that time. It is significant, however, to realize that Foulhouze, from the early days of his administration, considered the Supreme Council structure as possibly being limited to state boundaries just as Grand Lodges.

52. This account can not be confirmed in totality by any existing official record, but is recounted in an old unsigned handwritten paper located in the New Orleans Scottish Rite Library and Museum. In the notes of the 1859 *A Masonic Trial in New Orleans,* Charles Laffon de Laébat writes of the event: "... An opportunity offered and that was the address of Ill:. Bro. Chas. Claiborne who, instead of arguing the point at issue, that is, the merits and demerits of the 20 articles, amused himself by ridiculing the masonic costumes of Mr. Foulhouze. Mr. Foulhouze was stung to the quick and swore, in leaving the hall, that he had done with Masonry! He sent in his letter of resignation on the 30th of July 1853." page 43.

53. Alain Bernheim located the Minutes of the Supreme Council of Louisiana from its creation to 15 February 1847 in the BN in Paris in 1987. This writer located the Minutes of the Supreme Council of Louisiana from the election

of Charles Claiborne to the Concordat of 1855 in the Library of the New Orleans Scottish Rite Bodies in 1994.

54. *Official Bulletin VIII* 1886 p 536.

55. Foulhouze, *Historical Inquiry* 78. *The Masonic Delta*, August 1857 & March 1858. Charles Laffon de Ladébat, Translator, *A Masonic Trial in New Orleans (Lamarre's Defense)* (New Orleans, J. Lamarre, 1858) 43-44. Note: *A Masonic Trial in New Orleans* was written by Joseph Lamarre and originally published in French. The work was translated into English and republished that same year. The name of the translator is not given in this work. Charles Laffon de Ladébat states on page 83 of *Dissection of the Manifesto of Mr. Charles Bienienu* (New Orleans: privately published, 1858) that he was the translator for Lamarre' work and author of the notes in that book.

56. *The Masonic Delta* August 1857.

57. Ladébat, *A Masonic Trial in New Orleans* page 43.

58. Michael R. Poll, *In His Own (w)Rite*, (New Orleans, LA Cornerstone Book Publishers, 2011) "Albert Pike, His Addrtess before the Grand Consistory of Louisiana" page 5.

59. *The Masonic Delta* November 1857.

60. Felix Garcia, Lucien Hermann.

61. John Henry Holland.

62. Jean Lamothe & Robert Preaux.

63. Ramon Vionnet & Stephen Herriman.

64. François Meilleur and Charles Murian.

65. Jean B. Faget, Jean J.E. Massicott, Romain Brugier and Joseph Lisbony.

66. The revived New Orleans Council's monthly publication.

67. *The Masonic Delta* February 1858.

68. Although Pike was elected an Active Member in March, it was not until 7 July that Mackey would send the official general notification of his election. Harris, Carter *History* 260. Mackey would, however, inform Claude Samory of Pike's election on 8 May 1859. *Official Bulletin VIII*, 544.

69. Foulhouze's *Historical Inquiry* can not be viewed as an English translation of his *Mémoire à Consulter*. Upon examination by Alain Bernheim, it has been determined that the *Historical Inquiry*, while closely following *Mémoire à Consulter*, has enough significant changes to consider it a rewrite rather than a translation.

70. Scot, *Outline*. 4.

71. *The Masonic Delta* September 1859.

72. The *Masonic Delta* April 1860.

73. Lobingier, *Supreme Council*, 249.

74. Original document in the George Longe Collection in the Amistad Research Center at Tulane University, New Orleans, Louisiana.

75. Photocopy reproduction of the minutes in *The Perfect Ashlar* (publication of the Supreme Council of Louisiana) October 1969.

76. The *Bulletin* replaced *The Masonic Delta* in 1869 as the official publication of the Supreme Council of Louisiana.
77. Eugene Chassaignac *Bulletin* (New Orleans, A. Simon, 1869) 28.
78. Carter, *History* 431.
79. Foulhouze Secession Papers, 1875, Court House Pointe a la Hashe, Louisiana.

"WHENCE CAME YOU?"
by John L. Belanger, P.M.
Past Master, Louisiana Lodge of Research

Daily this question is asked by Masons without the slightest thought as to its real meaning. "Whence came you?" Who can really answer the question?

Equally baffling and profound is the question "What came you here to do?"

Simple as these questions appear, they search every nook and cranny and sound every depth of every philosophy, every mythology, every theology, and every religion that has ever been propounded anywhere by anybody at any time to explain human life.

In my opinion each person may have his own answer to "Whence Came you". However, your ideas may change after you read this paper. We must first start off to understand our roots "**Operative Masonry**":

In the early part of the 20th century two Masonic writers caused a minor ripple to disturb the placid waters of English freemasonry, and Masonic research in particular. The men concerned were Clement Edwin Stretton, a consultant engineer who lived in Leicester and wrote hundreds of book, academic papers and newspaper articles concerning railways and freemasonry; and John Yarker, who lived in Manchester and wrote even more books, academic papers and newspaper articles, but is now best remembered for one book in particular, *The Arcane Schools*, published in 1909, which is a giant of a book! It is impossible in a paper as short as this to do justice to the background and commitment of these two men, so it is hoped that it will be sufficient if anyone seeking further information is simply directed to the Internet or their nearest Masonic library. Both, however, eventually attained high rank, although both were subjected to personal criticism and, in my opinion, died disappointed men.

The cause which united them was their firm belief that modern speculative freemasonry did not suddenly emerge in 1717, which some would like us to believe, but was the linear descendant of operative freemasonry (and 'Guild' masonry in particular) which had been around for hundreds of years. Their reasons for being so certain were that, as a boy, Stretton had undergone training as a guild operative mason in a quarry in Derbyshire, and Yarker had known operative masons personally, some of whom had been operative masons for generations. To a large extent, both of these claims have been verified. Stretton claimed to have been sent for training to a Tor Quarry in Cromford, and it has been confirmed that, at the period quoted, there *was* a Tor Quarry in Cromford. He also claimed to have been indentured by someone named Montford or Mountford, and there *was* a Rev. Mountford living in the area at that time, who had a school for the training of boys in certain crafts. Yarker claimed that he knew an operative mason by the name of Eaton, who was a member of St. Ninian's Lodge, and the Secretary of St. Ninian's Lodge No. 66 (S.C.) has confirmed that there had been Eatons in that lodge for several generations, all of whom had been operative masons, and the last-named of which had joined that lodge from Ashton under Lyme, near to where Yarker lived.)

With Stretton as the leader, they then revived two former Guild Lodges (i.e. Leicester Lodge No. 91 and Mount Bardon Lodge No. 110) and used one to work the old operative ceremonies and the other to serve as a sort of Correspondence Circle, with the intention of attracting members. In this they succeeded for, by 1907, Mount Bardon Lodge had eighty-two members, many of whom were distinguished in various walks of life as well as in freemasonry, and more than a few who lived abroad, e.g. Isaac Henry Vrooman Jnr. and Charles Hope Merz who lived in the USA , John Gavin Purser who lived in Ireland, and S. Clifton Bingham who lived in Christchurch, New Zealand.

The cause of their enthusiasm for operative masonry was that they both considered it superior to speculative freemasonry, which they claimed was a pale imitation of the other, and some of those differences arose from the fact that , in Guild masonry:

Lodges were presided over by three Grand Master Masons.

Members sat in a lodge which was orientated the opposite way from normal, with the three Grand Master Masons sitting in the West.

Its members operated on a 7-degree system, the two poles of which were indentured apprentices as 1° and the three Grand Master Masons as VII°.

Apprentices were indentured at the age of 14 and had to prove their ability by 'test pieces' as they progressed through a 7-year system of training.

Lodges had existed for hundreds of years and used methods which were universal.

Lodges were known as 'Assemblages' throughout England, and some of them had an underground vault, with a plumb-line reaching down 'from Heaven' and a letter 'G' in the ceiling, denoting Geometry. There was also a central pedestal in the vault, which stood on seven steps, denoting the Seven Liberal Arts and Sciences.

Finally, that it was the operative masons who built St. Paul's Cathedral under Sir Christopher Wren, who was himself an operative mason.

All of these claims have been scrutinized as a result of which it can be confirmed that:

The Operative lodges *were* presided over by three Grand Master Masons each of whom carried a rod of either 3,4 or 5 units in length so that, by working together and using Pythagoras's Theorem, they could produce perfect right-angled triangles, which are vital to the stability of any structure. In fact, the three Grand Master Masons did all their work as a triad, thus giving rise to the "Rule of Three". Furthermore, York Lodge No.236 still has one of those rods in its archives, which bears the names John Barron, William Barron and John Drake, the date 1663, and the word 'Yorke'. If further proof is needed, one has only to look at the Orders of the Royal and Select Masters, or the Allied Masonic Degrees, both of which acknowledge their operative origins and, in some of their ceremonies, are presided over by three officers in the same way as the three Grand Master Masons.

As far as the orientation of lodges is concerned, it is my belief that all lodges should be orientated west-to-east, because that would be in full accord with Chapter 1 of the Book of Kings and Chapter 2 of the Book of Chronicles which explain that the entrance to the Temple was in the east. Besides, how else can a Master of any kind see the rising sun, his Senior Warden see the setting sun, and the Junior Warden see the sun at its meridian?

The idea of a seven-fold system of degrees is not as ridiculous as it at first seems, especially if the 1st and 2nd degrees are equated to the Craft; the 3rd, 4th and 5th degrees are equated to the Mark, the 6th degree to the Harodim or Past Master's degree, and the 7th degree to the Royal Arch. All those degrees were worked in operative lodges, and later in lodges under the Grand Lodge of All England (i.e. the Antients).

Apprentices *were* indentured at 14 and that is now more a matter of record than a tale of something which might or might not have happened. In that connection, Robert Whitfield's *History of the Lodge of Industry No. 48* (which was originally an operative lodge) is relevant, as that particular lodge continued to indenture young apprentices right up to and including 1775, by which time it had become a regular lodge administered by the Grand Lodge of England.

There can be no doubt that operative lodges existed for hundreds of years, and that is proved by the existence of so many copies of the Ancient Charges which were used in initiation ceremonies. And that they used methods which were universal would seem to be proved by the fact that the architects of Ancient Egypt were sometimes referred to as 'rope stretchers' because they used ropes knotted into lengths of 3,4 and 5 units in the same way as the three Grand Master Masons used their rods measuring 3,4 and 5 units, to create right-angled triangles.

In some places the Guild of Operative Masons built a vault underneath their lodge, with a plumb-line reaching down from Heaven, and a letter G in the ceiling, and an underground vault with a central pedestal, would now seem undeniable given the advent of the Royal and Select Masters and the Allied Masonic Degrees, both of which depend on those things for their continued existence. Underground vaults are also common in Royal Arch temples, and were illustrated on the Tracing Boards which were at one time used in Royal Arch ceremonies.

It *was* the operative masons who built St. Paul's Cathedral, and the architect *was* Sir Christopher Wren, who *was* an operative mason. This is proved by two plaques within the Cathedral, one of which commemorates 'Sir Christopher Wren – founder of this church', and another which reads 'Remember the men who made shapely the stones of St. Paul's Cathedral 1675-1708. Edward Strong, Thomas Strong, and all who labored with them. This tablet was erected by the Worshipful Company of Masons'. Both Strongs were operative masons from Gloucestershire who served the Company of Masons with distinction. The most compelling evidence in support of Sir Christopher Wren as a mason is provided by Professor Allan Beaver who, in a paper delivered in 2008, wrote that "The facts related form an evidential framework in which 70 originators, writing independently over a period of 130 years, cannot possibly have colluded. It borders on the ridiculous to cast doubt on evidence, which has survived over 300 years, that Sir Christopher Wren was a Freemason' and he concludes his paper with the comment that "the stench of unhealthy skepticism has pervaded Masonic research for far too long".

Having explained the above, Stretton and Yarker's next step was to intensify their public-speaking engagements on the subject of operative freemasonry, and to increase the amount of material they contributed to newspapers and Masonic publications. In fact, they attracted so much interest and attention that it was eventually decided to revive another of the old Guild lodges, and the one decided upon was in Westminster, London where, on 21st May 1913, Channel Row Assemblage was constituted at the Bijou Theatre, near Trafalgar Square. It was constituted by Dr. Thomas Carr who, by profession, was a doctor and barrister, and it had ten members.

It would be wrong to suggest that progress thereafter was meteoric, because it wasn't. For instance, Yarker died in 1913, Stretton died in 1915 (and Lodges 91 and 110 died with them) and two World Wars and The Depression took care of everything else. A second Assemblage *was* formed in the 1930s but that had to close-down in 1943 because it was located in an area to which – 'for security reason' - travel was prohibited (i.e. for the development of radar). Channel Row Assemblage continued, however, and gradually attracted a membership of the highest quality, including doctors, lawyers, university lecturers, actors, authors, army officers and politicians. The only real crisis which occurred, if it can be called a crisis, was in 1916 when there was a move to transform the Assemblage into 'The Worshipful Society of Free Masons for Operative Research'. But this was not agreed and it was resolved to continue 'working' the operative ceremonies rather than just talking about them. In due course, however, those members who were drawn to research did set up a society for that purpose which went by the name of the Masonic Study Society and, not surprisingly, most of its founder members were drawn from Channel Row Assemblage, such as Sir John Alexander Cockburn, J. S. M. Ward, Henry T. Cart De Lafontaine, Rt. Hon. Sir Frederick Pollock, Bernard H. Springett, Samuel Blaze Wilkinson, Dudley P. Hutchings, and Langford H. MacKelchen . The close connection between the Operatives and the Masonic Study Society continues to this day.

Eventually, some time after the second World War, the operatives did take off again, by then as a national organization under the lengthy title of the 'Worshipful Society of Free Masons, Rough Masons, Wallers, Slaters, Paviors, Plaisterers and Bricklayers' (which was the name under which the Guild operatives of Durham were Chartered in the 1638). To most people 'though, they were (and still are) usually referred to as 'the Operatives'. So, calculating from 1913 when they started; by 1943 there were two Assemblages, by 1963 there were three, by 1973 there were six, by 1983 there were eleven, by 1993 there were thirty-four, by 2003 there were sixty, and by 2013 (the society's Centenary year) we will have in excess of one hundred Assemblages. That is certain because we already have Assemblages in England, France, Belgium, Spain, Canada, Brazil, India, China, Australia, New Zealand, Malaysia and shortly (in August this year) in South Africa and we have already been notified of further interest and enthusiasm in some areas where they have already requested more Assemblages. One country, of course, seems to be conspicuously absent from that list, but that isn't because no one this side of the Atlantic is interested in operative freemasonry but because, for over ten years, freemasons from the USA have been regularly making the long journey to and from an Assemblage in Canada in order to progress as operatives and ultimately have their own Assemblage. But I shouldn't provoke you any further about this because, in reality, that objective has already been achieved and, in 2008, Bryn Athyn Quarry Assemblage was constituted in Allentown, Pennsylvania. So, the USA *does* now has an Assemblage and is not really missing from the list at all. And, if you would care to be brought totally up-to-date on that subject, only one month ago, three more Assemblages were constituted in the States, which were Solar White Quarry Assemblage in Monroe, North Carolina; Texas State Capitol Assemblage in San Antonio; and Trinity Church Assemblage in New York, so the U.S. is now doing very well indeed

If, however, you will permit me a moment of irony, you might like to note that, in 1912, i.e. one year before the formation of Channel Row Assemblage in London, Dr. Charles Hope Merz, a distinguished American freemason who was mentioned at the start of this talk, was authorized by Stretton to open an operative Assemblage in Sandusky,

Ohio and made a start by creating the necessary administrative team to do it, with J. Raymond Shute as the Grand Clerk. Sadly, the War got in the way, so it never came to anything. But, if it had, things could be very different today. If it had taken off, the chances are that today, the United States would be the dominating country instead of England!

Either way round, I do not think that Brothers Stretton and Yarker have a lot to be disappointed about. After an uncertain and controversial start, the Society they created has stood the test of time, and that is something they should feel good about. The existence of such a Society constantly causes its members to think about and question their origins, and that can only be good for freemasonry.

Now with this information you may be able to know the answer to the question of "Whence came you" yes, you guessed it "**Operative Masonry.**"

" PERSONAL INTEGRITY"
THE CORNERSTONE OF MASONIC PHILOSOPHY
by Clayton J. Borne, III, P.G.M. (Louisiana)
Worshipful Master, Louisiana Lodge of Research

In November, 2006 at the 8th World Conference of Regular Masonic Grand Lodges, I had the honor of presenting a paper entitled, "Relevancy of Freemasonry in the Twenty-first Century", wherein it was presented that the universal appeal of our fraternal brotherhood over the ages was the direct result of our convictions relative to our Spiritual beliefs, namely the fundamental principles of "Monotheism", defined as the oneness of God; "Transfiguration", defined as mans ability to return to the Spirit state upon death; and "Transformation", defined as the molding of man from a rough stone to a higher State of Spiritual Reality. The Masonic Philosophy demands of each Brother, to individually commit to that spiritual discipline, and have him understand that collectively he has an opportunity to contribute to a cause that leads to a more ordered society and the betterment of mankind. The paper concluded with the conclusion that our fundamental principles and their significance in society are just as relevant today as they were to our ancient brothers.

Accepting this conclusion as the premise for this paper and extrapolating the cause and effect relationship forward in time, what is true is that civilized society and mankind in general will measure the dynamics of our Spiritual Brotherhood not by its idealistic objectives, but whether the Masonic philosophy is truly alive and evident in the lives of each of our brothers. In other words if instead of integrity they see hypocrisy, instead of truth they see prevarication, instead of honesty they see deception; our footprints on the pages of time will be tarnished. Where our history evidences a God Centered Life adorned in a cloak of charity, brazened by badges of truth, honor and courage, the 21st century will continue to see men drawn to our lodges, as the Brotherhood and its destiny is truly a reflection of who we are and all that we do.

As a predicate to this paper I ask each of my brothers the question, "Why do we, as a brotherhood, believe that belief in a Supreme Being is necessary for a personal transformation in our lives and ultimately necessary for the development of a disciplined yet free society?" As an extension of that thought," Why is a belief in a Supreme Being essential to the landmarks of our fraternity and sacred to the ritual of our "Regular" Masonic Lodges? The answer is fundamental to understanding the Masonic Philosophy or the Masonic Way of Life.

Exactly how were we able to affirm a belief in a Supreme Being and what effect did that acceptance have on our lives? Have we truly challenged the concept of the "Being behind Reality" and its effect on the men that we are? Did the Masonic initiation ritual enhance your conviction and your commitment to spiritual growth? Philosophers over the ages have challenged this basic concept and pushed mankind to investigate more specific questions. What is the nature of God and how is God related to the universe? Is God a force responsible for creation? What is the true concept of God? Is it possible to even come to a knowledge of God? And for us, as Masons, why was it essential to the tenants of our brotherhood that we affirm the concept before gaining admission? Why have we severed communications with those Grand Lodges that believe it is no longer essential to the Masonic discipline to embrace a belief in a Supreme Being?

Knowledge of God

The concept challenged by many early philosophers and historians which is fundamental to each of our most basic beliefs is, "How do we as humans come to a knowledge of God and why is it important?" Further for the purpose of this paper what effect does this academic inquiry have on our Masonic Brotherhood, its spiritual pursuits and objectives?

After much research, self reflection and thought, it is my sincere belief that a finite creature, such as man, to come to a knowledge of an infinite creature or being such as God, is on its surface impossible. The reason: man as a finite creature can not truly understand or comprehend the limitless concepts such as eternity or infinity. Despite many brilliant, philosophers, allegations to the contrary finite man conceptionally defines everything in terms of or with limits.

GOD HOWEVER MOST DEFINITELY CAN BE KNOWN. God is known to the extent that his nature would demand it be revealed. That is, in the ways God would choose to reveal himself to his created. An example would be found in our perception and knowledge of nature. As a Christian the revelation would be the embodiment and person of Jesus Christ. There are others. Only in the revelation is a finite knowledge of God possible. By his creation God or the Creator becomes the principal of the Universe. God is the whole of his creation: God is truly the "Grand Architect of the Universe".

Effect on Man of a Belief in God

I submit that the reason that a belief in God is essential for our Spiritual Brotherhood is because of our fraternity's conviction and purpose to aggressively encourage the development of the spiritual nature of man, knowing well that our object over time is the creation and development of a self disciplined society. That development must of necessity begin with each of us personally and its success measured by our individual spiritual advancement. When viewed collectively this discipline creates dynamic lodges. The obvious question becomes, how does this process individually and collectively take place? Exactly what are the results and are they truly in harmony with what we believe are our personal life goals and objectives?

Very simply a belief in God has an immediate and direct bearing on our values and convictions. Those disciplines have a direct effect on our behavior. The motivation is the acceptance or belief opens the door to the spirit life after death and our ability as finite creatures to pass upon death to an infinite state. Exactly how does this intellectual affirmation or belief transform each of us, and is our Masonic Fraternity doing its part in simulating this growth?

Understanding that once man had a conviction or belief in God, it created, in addition to the most basic concept of survival which dominated and existed in a non orderly barbaric society, a true purpose for life. Belief in a creator, God, transforms man from a rude, self centered, savage state into a creature with a more civilized meaningful purpose. That objective or hope is to unify himself ultimately with his creator with the sincere desire of returning to the spirit or infinite state always with eternity in view. It begins to change our convictions and beliefs and ultimately our lives. How do this acceptance of God and this life changing process take place?

Our Masonic Brotherhood teaches and encourages a philosophy of self transformation and the development of a character that recognizes the need to subordinate personal gain and self interest to the greater good of society. The transformation of the finite spirit in each of us demands a reassessment of the most basic concepts of life in order to give priority and meaning to the fundamental concepts of goodness which are absolutely necessary for the advancement of mankind in a free society, which society evidences an individual and collective self discipline to maintain and insure order. That order has a fundamental principle; that principle is "Truth". Our Brotherhood embraces truth as the heart and soul of each and every virtue. As Masons we advocate a virtuous life. It logically follows that a virtuous life results in a life of integrity.

I submit that individual integrity is the essential element in a social structure or order that cultivates and encourages individual and collective freedom and liberty. It insures a disciplined society that cultivates in a secure way the collective peaceful advancement of humanity. In general, where personal integrity is lacking laws become problematic and of little value. This is why we as Masons mandate this unselfish discipline for all of humanity, especially our Brotherhood. How exactly do we individually achieve these idealistic principles and what is our responsibility as Masonic mentors, especially to the Entered Apprentice who is still trying to understand himself and the confusion of the world in which he lives. It begins with a belief in God.

Masonic Ideals

As we strive to cultivate integrity in our personal lives and collectively in our spiritual brotherhood, our efforts meet with constant resistance. As appalling as it may be realistically, society today is a reflection of disrespect, an unappreciative and uncaring disease that migrates into all aspects of our respective culture. The cure as with all other social problems is education.

The Masonic ideals and their influence on society through the ages have been exerted in no better or nobler purpose or cause than the ageless struggle by the Brotherhood for "Liberty, Equality and Fraternity" and ultimately a secure freedom for society. Our Fraternity through the ages has been the champions of the oppressed people with the object being the emancipation of mankind from every form of tyranny. Within our lodges Liberty or Freedom, especially in thought, was freely encouraged. That freedom based on these principles made it possible for the natural progression of a transformed life.

The humanist philophsy so prevalent in society poses obstructions to our Masonic ideals. The basic concept of Liberty has always had an aggressive enemy. It is the self centered, selfish concept of entitlement. The entitlement belief is the direct result of the modernist doctrine that there is no rational basis for values. Despite our Masonic brotherhood's continued efforts to promote integrity, the value system of society has been eroded. Much of society values become problematic, in other words nothing is truly good or bad. It's all a matter of opinion. We must of necessity ask then how and why have principals? Do as you please or whatever you can rationalize as being right. Without the liberty to choose our own actions and make our own choices, we lose the qualities of responsibility that make us uniquely human. It is only when people do the right thing freely can we have confidence in their character. If they act out of principles such as truth, benevolence, productiveness as taught in our lodges then we know their actions resulted from good character and the principle of liberty is preserved.

Integrity

The world in which we now live is dramatically changing. Idealistic principles are important to fewer and fewer people. We demand of our leaders, honesty, but we don't really expect them to be honest. Our societies have become problematic where honesty becomes relative and rationalization of all conduct is the norm. We are often saying that our communities are civilized societies of law, but to often laws are broken and then attempts are made to justify the actions. That logic is corruptive, destructive but most importantly contagious.

Prevarication or lying has infected our culture. The generation of today lies without thought. They lie for no apparent reason. Recent surveys state that 90% of society lies in some manner frequently. Truthfulness is no longer a virtue people try to adopt for their lives. Conversely Masonic Philosophers and our Masonic Ritual of instruction view truth as a divine attribute and as we have previously stated truth should be at the heart of each and every virtue.

Marriage and family are no longer sacred institutions. Infidelity is common place. The work ethics of our forefathers are disappearing from society. Procrastination at the workplace is common with no respect or appreciation given to the employment. Society says that it wants respect but modern man's life experiences evidence a serious lack of it. The lack of respect in society is the end result of a lack of purpose, discipline and moral commitment. These are the very ideals that we as Masons, fight to preserve.

A brother whose life evidences qualities of honesty, discipline and courage is proof of a transformed life that has earned respect. His life embodies an individual quest and a determined search for light. It is a fraternal concept shared with our brothers of like mind. This writer submits that the attraction, the spiritual reward, the ultimate objective of our spiritual brotherhood is the character which is the epitome of all virtue, namely "Integrity". In general the quality is defined as our ability to naturally embrace a way of life with moral and ethical principles. Its presence in each of our lives will be the attribute that will continue to draws good men to our Lodges.

The driving force of our Masonic Fraternity is to instill in each of our brothers a mission to create within each man that knocks at our door of our lodges a thirst for integrity. That desire can only be quenched by a commitment to those moral principles or goals in each of our lives. We must teach that truth, honesty and moral principles are of prime importance. The newly made Brother should be instructed to subsequently understand that a man of integrity is unimpeachable; he is steadfast; his word is his bond. He is never critical of others, even those in which he is in opposition. He restrains his emotions or passions. He is reliable and is one to always pay his debt. He should stand upon principle no matter what the consequence whether alone or in a crowd.

Concluion

To the entered apprentice and his search for light, "Integrity" and its Masonic ideals are but idealistic concepts although often cognitively embraced; it is rarely evident in his life. The apprentice, as he begins his transformation, begins to understand that a person of integrity is a person that thrives for consistency of principal and that principle translates to living the ideals. In other words, ideals such as Truth, Honesty, Charity and Moral Discipline are no longer problematic nor are they mere idealistic principles. They are to become a true way of life. Our young brother is developing a philosophy of purpose.

The Mason begins to understand that the fullness of life is found in that consistency and he is made aware of the rewards and blessings of living a life with ideals as guiding principles. He realizes in a more profound way that his integrity is defined and is the result of choices made repeatedly in his daily life. The brother begins to realize that the joy in this life's reality is in the journey, the journey with ideals, the journey with purpose.

Our Spiritual Brotherhood is committed to the concept that all of mankind is entitled to be enlightened and that process begins with a God centered life. It develops respect for the laws of society, but more important to us as Masons, it is a self imposed discipline. A discipline that through its ideal generates unbelievable rewards: Freedom of thought, Freedom of religion, Freedom of Speech, Freedom to hold diverse beliefs are to name but a few.

Where the dignity of man, especially within the Brotherhood, is measured by the integrity of his life, that dignity becomes an ideal of respect; that ideal then can be freely expected and freely given. It is basic to the tenant of our fraternity.

Collectively we as brothers have the opportunity to make the world in which we live a better place, a place of integrity where our Masonic ideals do in fact become a way of life.

ESOTERISM AND FREEMASONRY
by Michael R. Poll, P.M.
Secretary, Louisiana Lodge of Research

Introduction

Alice came to a fork in the road. "Which road do I take?" she asked.
"Where do you want to go?" responded the Cheshire cat.
"I don't know," Alice answered.
"Then," said the cat, "it doesn't matter."

~ Lewis Carroll, *Alice in Wonderland*

Esoterism and Freemasonry - well, that's certainly a combination to strike fear in the hearts of the unsuspecting. For those who see Freemasonry as a nice group of pals who gather together every few weeks, do a little ritual and share good conversations with a hot meal, the concept of Freemasonry having anything to do with esotericism might be quite foreign, quite implausible.

So, what is esotericism? For that matter, what is Freemasonry? We'll try to explore these questions within the following pages and express some thoughts on the matter. Esotericism might well be a stranger to many readers, but once introduced and you get to know it a bit, you may find it to be a very good friend.

But, there is no need to push or struggle with foreign concepts. Not every path is for every traveler. This is not a book of laws. No one should ever expect another to accept what is, for them, unacceptable. This is a book of thoughts and ideas written only with the hope of assisting you in a better understating of esoterism and its relationship with Freemasonry - nothing more, nothing less.

By the way, if you are an alchemist or a serious student of the deeper aspects of Mystical Masonry, this book might seem a bit elementary to you. It's true, it is. The goal of this book is not to explain what is already known to the serious esoteric Mason. The goal is to introduce esotericism, explain to the uninformed reader some of its connection to Freemasonry and guide them to additional information on the subject.

As in all things Masonic, the goal is the search for more Light.

What is Esoterism?

"When the student is ready, the master appears."

~ Buddhist Proverb

Can you imagine somehow going back in time to the Middle Ages, standing in a crowd of people and then receiving a call on your cell phone? How do you believe the people around you would react? Humans evaluate and respond to situations based on their experience. We all have heard cell phones ring and someone answering a call. We may not know exactly how the thing works, but we have experience in the matter and recognize it as a common communication device. But how would someone in the Middle Ages, with their life experiences, view such an event? Would we be seen as some sort of magician who was using, maybe, evil powers? Most likely. Would we generate fear in those around us and be in some physical danger? Most probably. Cell phones did not exist in the Middle Ages. Nothing like them existed. They would have been viewed as something beyond reason and totally impossible to exist within the normal manner of life. It would be a magical device. At that time in history, whatever was viewed as existing beyond the realm of the familiar or normal life was the unknown, the esoteric, the dangerous, the magical ... the evil. It was the only way such things could be explained.

Claude Bernard tells us: "Man can learn nothing except by going from the known to the unknown." Even when we consider the powerful fear of the unknown, human quest for knowledge has always existed and was never, for long, denied. We were and are curious beings. In the very early days of mankind, lightening striking a tree must have been a terrifying event and the tree must have been viewed as dangerous long after the strike. But, this would not have stopped a curious few from approaching the "dangerous" tree and touching it. Maybe they could not properly answer why they did such a foolish thing, but they simply *had* to do it. They *had* to reach out

The end of the Dark Ages was an ignorant, violent and fearful time. If you did something to create fear in another you would most likely face harm - and, fear of magic or the unknown/unexplainable was a profound fear. The dawn of the Middle Ages saw the Church as the proper source (by force) of all acceptable information, knowledge and answers. To seek answers for what was not explained, or beyond what was given, by the Church put your very life in danger. Yet there were those who did just that. They questioned information or answers given by the Church. They sought to learn for themselves and reach beyond the limited teachings of the Church. They knowingly sought knowledge at the risk of their lives. They simply *had* to do it. They *had* to reach out. These seekers of Light gave birth to what we know today as esoterism, but really, also medicine, science and a host of other fields. In the words of Albert Einstein, "The most beautiful thing we can experience is the mystical. It is the source of all true art and science."

Esoteric knowledge or teachings have come to be known as the private or inner teachings that were not available to everyone. In most all cases, these teachings were carefully guarded as to be associated with them could be an actual death sentence. Small groups of students would gather to explore all aspects of themselves and the world around them in total secrecy. Vows and oaths were often required of new members in order to protect them all and to better the chance of the continuation of the group.

It was in this atmosphere that the seeds of what we have today as Freemasonry were sown. How old is Freemasonry? Before you can begin to answer that question you must answer, "What is Freemasonry?" In his classic "The Secret Teachings of All Ages," Manly P. Hall writes:

> "The sanctum sanctorum of Freemasonry is ornamented with the gnostic jewels of a thousand ages; its rituals ring with the divinely inspired words of seers and sages. A hundred religious have brought their gifts of wisdom to its altar; arts and sciences unnumbered have contributed to its symbolism. Freemasonry is a world-wide university, teaching the liberal arts and sciences of the soul to all who will hearken to its words. Its chairs are seats of learning and its pillars uphold an arch of universal education. Its trestleboards are inscribed with the eternal verities of all ages and upon those who comprehend its sacred depths has dawned the realization that within the Freemasonic Mysteries lie hidden the long-lost arcana sought by all peoples since the genesis of human reason.

"The philosophic power of Freemasonry lies in its symbols—its priceless heritage from the Mystery schools of antiquity. In a letter to Robert Freke Gould, Albert Pike writes:

'It began to shape itself to my intellectual vision into something more imposing and majestic, solemnly mysterious and grand. It seemed to me like the Pyramids in their loneliness, in whose yet undiscovered chambers may be hidden, for the enlightenment of coming generations, the sacred books of the Egyptians, so long lost to the world; like the Sphynx half buried in the desert. In its symbolism, which and its spirit of brotherhood are its essence, Freemasonry is more ancient than any of the world's living religions. It has the symbols and doctrines which, older than himself, Zarathustra inculcated; and seemed to me a spectacle sublime, yet pitiful—the ancient Faith of our ancestors holding out to the world its symbols once so eloquent, and mutely and in vain asking for an interpreter. And so I came at last to see that the true greatness and majesty of Freemasonry consist in its proprietorship of these and its other symbols; and that its symbolism is its soul.'

"Though the temples of Thebes and Karnak be now but majestic heaps of broken and time-battered stone, the spirit: of Egyptian philosophy still marches triumphant through the centuries. Though the rock-hewn sanctuaries of the ancient Brahmins be now deserted and their carvings crumbled into dust, still the wisdom of the Vedas endures. Though the oracles be silenced and the House of the Mysteries be now but rows of ghostly columns, still shines the spiritual glory of Hellas with luster undiminished. Though Zoroaster, Hermes, Pythagoras, Plato, and Aristotle are now but dim memories in a world once rocked by the transcendency of their intellectual genius, still in the mystic temple of Freemasonry these god-men live again in their words and symbols; and the candidate, passing through the initiations, feels himself face to face with these illumined hierophants of days long past."

When the little groups of knowledge seekers illegally gathered, they could not speak or teach freely. They could not, even within their own group, provide open educational material for fear that it would be discovered and result in imprisonment or death for all. So, they employed the use of symbols to teach. It was not a new way of teaching. Teaching by symbols had been in use since the dawn of mankind. But, it was effective. Profound teachings could be presented by the use of symbols and those uneducated in the meaning of the symbols would be able to see nothing of what was being taught. It not only was an effective way to teach, but it provided security.

Freemasonry teaches by the use of symbols because its roots are in the very esoteric groups that used this method to teach. Esoterism is not a foreign subject to Freemasonry but is as much a part of the fabric of Freemasonry as is initiation.

"Who is more foolish, the child afraid of the dark or the man afraid of the light?"

~ Maurice Freehill

Living in a World of Change

"One of the strange things about living in the world is that it is only now and then one is quite sure one is going to live forever and ever and ever. One knows it sometimes when one gets up at the tender solemn dawn-time and goes out and stands alone and throws one's head far back and looks up and up and watches the pale sky slowly changing and flushing and marvelous unknown things happening until the East almost makes one cry out and one's heart stands still at the strange unchanging majesty of the rising of the sun-which has been happening every morning for thousands and thousands and thousands of years. One knows it then for a moment or so..."

~ Frances Burnett

For all our great achievements, man is a lonely, simple being. We are bound to all of the laws of nature just as the most uncomplicated and basic forms of life. When it rains, we get wet. When the temperature drops, we become cold. For all our self-professed intelligence we live at the mercy of the elements and are bound to laws that we hardly understand much less control. We are slaves in the guise of masters.

But, we do have a great ability. It is called free will. We have the power to use our mind and our actions (to the extent of their limits) in a manner of our choosing. We don't have to think evil. We don't have to do evil - unless that is what we choose to do. We have the ability to make the choice. We can change how we think. We can improve our minds. Or, we can do nothing. Mahatma Gandhi wrote, "We must become the change we want to see." It does not best serve us to expect the world to change to suit our fancy. It also does not mean that if all around us is unsatisfactory, we must change to suit the fancy of others. We have the right to refuse change forced upon us. Gandhi also wrote, "You can chain me, you can torture me, you can even destroy this body, but you will never imprison my mind." There is a balance we must achieve and a responsibility we must assume that goes along with free-will.

When we boil Freemasonry down to its most basic element, we find a very simple message: "make yourself better." Such a statement can, however, be likened to the phrase "be happy." It sounds easy enough, but how do you do it? How do you know when you are "better?" What is "better?" What seems to be an uncomplicated message becomes difficult to put into practice, even to understand. Such is the nature of symbolism.

We can start on the path of symbolic understanding by looking at nature. If you look at a beautiful mountain stream, you can find more than beauty. You can find illusion (often, the guardian of symbolism). Flowing water goes around a large rock in the stream. The illusion is that the rock is the master. What we believe to be truth is the sight of the water yielding to the rock and being forced to flow around it. We see this and accept it as truth. Our error is that we determined "the truth" before we gathered all the facts. In time, gentle, flowing water can reduce the largest stone to a pebble. The rock is not the master. One lesson to learn is that what we see, hear, feel and believe might well prove to be something other than fact. We must train ourselves to withhold judgment.

In Freemasonry, a subtle lesson is taught early on by putting us in a position where we cannot depend on what we can see. We are forced to depend on others for guidance. We are also forced to use senses other than those we would normally rely upon. We must change in order to adapt to this new situation. The illusion is that we have been handicapped and deprived of receiving the full benefit that would have been afforded us if we had complete use of all of our senses. But the illusion masks the fact that we are forced to adapt to our condition precisely because we have been placed in such a state. We simply can't act or perform on our own. We need guidance.

The three degrees in Craft Masonry are often said to represent the three stages of human life: youth, adulthood and old age. How do we progress through these stages? We change. As children, we play, grow and learn. As adults, we put into practice what we have learned, and in old age we impart to others what we have learned. In each stage, we change in body and mind. It is the normal way of life. What would be abnormal is if no change took place.

Let's look again at the water and the rock, and see the apparent change. The gentle, flowing water cannot and does not break the rock by direct force. Water changes its direction and flows around the rock; in doing so, it also gradually affects change in the rock. The gentle pressures of the water force the rock to give way and reduce itself in size. Change is one of the unavoidable facts of all existence. Any attempt to avoid change only results in an unnatural waste of energy.

The lessons of Masonry are such that we must study them with a child's open and willing mind. In certain aspects of our teachings, we might remember we are told that it is not acceptable to bring "innovations" into the body of Masonry. An innovation is change. Are we being told that we cannot or should not change? Not at all.

As individuals, we change every day of our lives. We grow older, which brings physical and mental changes. We have no choice in these types of changes. We also have the option to make free-will choices in our lives. We might opt to eat a more healthful diet, to exercise, or in some way improve our lives. There are countless changes that we can choose. We also might make the decision not to make any free-will changes. It is our choice as individuals.

But when we speak of innovations in Masonry, we are speaking of something quite different. The innovations that are made in Masonry should never be the choice of any single individual. Changes should be the collective will of the membership. In Masonry it is the lodge, not the Worshipful Master, who decides the direction to be taken. The Worshipful Master only steers the ship in the desired direction.

In our Grand Lodges, we see change every year. We see resolutions presented and voted on. It is rare that a Grand Lodge will see no change whatsoever in its nature after a Grand Lodge session. Change is normal. Change is expected.

In Masonry, the changes we see in its nature often mirror the changes we see in wider society. Freemasons are part of society and we interact with others on a daily basis. It would be unnatural for us to be social outcasts. If we look back at Masonry 50 or 100 years ago, or even longer, we see that the nature of Masonry matched that of society in both simple matters of dress and deep social or philosophical issues. Even today, we see social difference in Masonry depending on the location of the lodge and its membership. In a large city, you might see lodge members dressing in a different manner than you would see in a small town. One is not right and the other wrong, they are just simple differences in the social norms of the areas.

When we look at society and speak of a large nation, it would be uninformed to not realize that society's concepts of what is acceptable and unacceptable vary from community to community. The overall social structure of a large area allows for change and variations within smaller areas. Speed limits might change from one place to another, as well as many other community-based laws, but where will you find murder legal? Society as a whole has limits as to what are acceptable standards.

Because Grand Lodges are sovereign and free to pass the rules and laws of their liking, it would seem highly improbable that you would find two Grand Lodges with exactly the same set of governing laws. If one Grand Lodge changed its laws to require all members to wear tuxedos to lodge, it might draw a level of interest from some other Grand Lodges, but that would be about it. If the same Grand Lodge removed the Volume of Sacred Law from its altars, then not only would this attract the attention of other Grand Lodges, but they would view this Grand Lodge as moving outside of what is today considered acceptable, and the breaking of fraternal relations with this jurisdiction might follow. By the same turn, if most Grand Lodges adopted a particular policy which they felt was extremely important, then those few Grand Lodges not adopting the policy might also be viewed as unacceptable or out of step.

Change is not the enemy of Masonry. Just as the water in a stream changes direction as it flows in and around various obstacles, so should we recognize that change is not only inevitable, but is in our best interest. In a storm, it is the strong, unyielding tree, not the flexible blade of grass, that is in most danger of breaking.

"What we think, we become." ~ Buddha

Moral Teachings and Symbolism

"Once, however, we have realised that God is just and that we are all partakers of the same nature, all equally His children, we shall perceive that we shall hardly be acting justly to our fellow men if we leave them behind in the race, and do not help and assist them so that all humanity may achieve the same goal."

~ J.S.M. Ward

Around the world, there are many different types of Freemasonry. By that, I mean the rituals that are used and practiced. While the words and activities of the craft degrees in the different rites vary, sometimes quite a bit, one common thread that runs through all of the various rites and rituals is the legend of Hiram. Now, before I say anything else, I have to throw in a disclaimer of sorts. Some time back I heard that a jurisdiction was thinking about removing the legend of Hiram from their ritual. As surprising as that information was, the reason behind their idea was even more remarkable. I was told that the reason for their wanting to remove this aspect of the ritual was because they could not establish that the legend of Hiram was a factual historical event. I was stunned. It is a symbolic story; a lesson. It is completely irrelevant if the story of Hiram is fact or fiction. We are not teaching a history class. The story is used as a vehicle to deliver lessons of virtue and morality. The lessons that are taught are what is important, not the factual nature of the story used to present the lessons.

So, with that disclaimer made, I'll continue with the story. The story takes place at the time of the building of King Solomon's Temple. We are taught that a great many operative Masons worked on the construction of the Temple. These Masons were guided in their work by three Grand Masters: King Solomon, King Hiram of Tyre and the lead architect, Hiram Abif. At some point, the three Grand Masters realized that a number of the craftsmen were performing their duties at such a high level of skill that it entitled them to special recognition. These craftsmen would be elevated to Master craftsmen.

Now, in today's Freemasonry, if we receive a degree, an office or position of importance, we're honored by that advancement. But, in reality, it means very little outside of our Masonic life. Our Freemasonry is Speculative Freemasonry, and it is something we do outside of our family life and livelihood. This was not the same with the old Operative Freemasons. Freemasonry *was* their livelihood. It was how they fed their family and paid their bills. Being advanced to the rank of Master was a big deal. Not only did it mean an elevation in their social status, it also meant a considerable pay increase. This advancement was a very important event in their life.

When the news of the pending advancements was made known, we can assume that considerable excitement and interest developed. It is because of the importance of these advancements to the lives of those receiving them that some concern among the Grand Masters developed. It seemed reasonable to put into place some sort of security measure so that individuals of low moral character could not assume rank for which they were not entitled. It was decided that a secret word would be given to all new Masters of the Craft so that they could prove their rank by the possession of this word. As a further security measure, it was decided that this word would not be given out to anyone unless all three Grand Masters were present and agreed to the investiture.

The story goes on that three craftsmen obviously realized that they would likely not be elevated to a higher rank and were very unhappy about it. They wanted this advancement - badly. So much did they want this advancement that they hatched a plan to steal this "secret word," move to another area and live their lives pretending to hold a rank they did not earn. They caught one of the Grand Masters alone and demanded that he tell them the secret word. When he refused, they roughed him up a bit. When the Grand Master still refused to give them the word, they became desperate. They made it clear to him that they were going to leave with either the word or him dead. At this point, the Grand Master had a choice. He could give them what they wanted, or he could risk death. Clearly, he took them seriously as his final words reflect acknowledgement of what he believed would happen, "Of my life you may deprive me; of my integrity, never!"

Think about what happened for a minute. There is something that I have been taught since childhood, and, most likely, you have also been taught. It is that if I am ever in a situation where someone threatens my life in a robbery attempt, I should give them whatever they want. Why didn't he? I was taught that nothing I have on me is worth risking my life. Why didn't he just give them this word and then he could live and go on with his life?

The lesson of integrity is involved not because of a robbery attempt, but because of an agreement that was made. This Grand Master agreed that he would not give the secret word to anyone unless certain conditions were met. Had these craftsmen attempted to simply rob him of some money, then it is reasonable that he would have freely exchanged whatever money he had on him for his life. But, what these men wanted was something completely different. They demanded that he violate an agreement, his word.

The Grand Master's final words need closer attention. He said, "Of my life you may deprive me ..." What does that mean? He clearly recognized that he was not in control of their actions. He could not make them spare his life or do anything at all. Taking his life was something that they would either do or not do and he had no control whatsoever over their actions. The only thing in which he had total control was *his* actions. They could take his life, but they could not take this word from him. He could only give it and that would be by his choice.

The Grand Master needed to determine what was of true value to him. He knew that we all live and die, but he also knew that how we live is up to us. To be robbed of some coins is no dishonor, but what of violating his word? What was that worth to him? He did not agree to only give the word when certain conditions were met *unless* his life was threatened or only on the third Tuesday of the month if there was a full Moon. He agreed to *not* give it unless these conditions were met. *Period*. If he gave the word to anyone and those conditions were not met then he would be violating his word. It did not matter if they offered him money, threatened him or anything else. He would either keep his word or break it.

In life we can gain or lose material things. Because of the twists and turns in life we can amass great wealth or lose everything we own. Many things can happen to us because we were either in the right place or the wrong place. But either we have integrity and honor, or we do not. We have it because it is our choice and we lose it by the same choice. Material things can be taken away from us and we might have no choice in the matter. But, not our integrity. We are the only ones who have the power to give our integrity away.

The Grand Master knew that we all live and die. He also knew that all of the magnificent structures that he helped create would mean nothing if his moral foundation was made of sand - void of integrity or honor. These men had the power to take his life, but they were powerless to make him live a life without integrity. This was the point of the story - to teach a life lesson of virtue and morality, not to simply provide a historical account. But, we should not believe that the story ends there.

The nature of symbolism is layered and often requires second and third looks to find deeper meanings. Just because we *believe* that we are acting with honor or integrity does not mean that this is actually the case. Let me give you an example.

A story from New Orleans in the early 1800's come to mind. There were two men who were standing outside the St. Louis Cathedral having a friendly conversation. The two men were facing each other. One of the men felt a bit uncomfortable in his position and moved just a bit to the left to reposition himself. When the man moved over, the other man winced in pain and looked shocked. In a sharp tone he demanded that the man return to his original position. The man who moved had no idea of what the other man was talking, but did not like his tone of voice. What neither man realized or considered was that the man who moved was considerably taller than the other man. In the position he was standing, he (unknown to either man) was standing right in a place where he was blocking the sun. When he moved a bit over, the sunlight hit the shorter man right in the eyes causing his painful reaction.

Neither man was of a mind to explain himself or ask too many questions of the other. Hot tempers took over and the friendly conversation was replaced by a very heated, nonsensical argument. And then it happened ... one man exclaimed that his "honor" had become compromised and "integrity" demanded satisfaction. He challenged the other man to a duel.

It was fortunate that neither man died in the duel, but one of them was shot in the arm. For the rest of his life, he lived with a useless arm as the result of the injury suffered in that duel. And for what? Honor? Integrity? One man move a bit and the other man had sun in his eyes. For that you shoot at each other?

What these men mistook for honor and integrity was pride, arrogance and vanity. These vices were disguised as, or mistaken for, virtues. There was no loss of honor in what happened and integrity demanded nothing in the way of a duel.

We must live our lives with honor and integrity. But, we must know what is a virtue and what is a vice disguised as virtue. It's not always as clear as we think. If anyone has ever told us that being a Mason is easy, then they misled us. There will be times when we find it most difficult to live up to our teachings. But, as we are so often told, it is the journey that is most important, not the final goal.

"Conscience is God's presence in man." ~ Emanuel Swedenborg

Alchemy

"The greatest discovery of my generation is that a human being can alter his life by altering his attitudes." ~ William James

When we speak of alchemy and Freemasonry together, it can be a flashpoint for argument. Masons sometimes view alchemy, especially when connected to Freemasonry, as something akin to booga booga nonsense. Alchemists are often viewed as nutty old men in long robes doing strange things all with the goal of swindling ignorant medieval royalty out of their wealth. Alchemists are often viewed as opportunistic con-men who played on the ignorance, superstition and greed of their victims.

Of alchemy and the old alchemists, Manly P. Hall writes in his classic "The Secret Teachings of all Ages":

"Is the transmutation of base metals into gold possible? Is the idea one at which the learned of the modern world can afford to scoff? Alchemy was more than a speculative art: it was also an operative art. Since the time of the immortal Hermes, alchemists have asserted (and not without substantiating evidence) that they could manufacture gold from tin, silver, lead, and mercury. That the galaxy of brilliant philosophic and scientific minds who, over a period of two thousand years, affirmed the actuality of metallic transmutation and multiplication, could be completely sane and rational on all other problems of philosophy and science, yet hopelessly mistaken on this one point, is untenable. Nor is it reasonable that the hundreds declaring to have seen and performed transmutations of metals could all have been dupes, imbeciles, or liars.

"Those assuming that all alchemists were of unsound mentality would be forced to put in this category nearly all the philosophers and scientists of the ancient and medieval worlds. Emperors, princes, priests, and common townsfolk have witnessed the apparent miracle of metallic metamorphosis. In the face of existing testimony, anyone is privileged to remain unconvinced, but the scoffer elects to ignore evidence worthy of respectful consideration. Many great alchemists and Hermetic philosophers occupy an honored niche in the Hall of Fame, while their multitudinous critics remain obscure. To list all these sincere seekers after Nature's great arcanum is impossible, but a few will suffice to acquaint the reader with the superior types of intellect who interested themselves in this abstruse subject.

"Among the more prominent names are those of Thomas Norton, Isaac of Holland, Basil Valentine (the supposed discoverer of antimony), Jean de Meung, Roger Bacon, Albertus Magnus, Quercetanus Gerber (the Arabian who brought the knowledge of alchemy to Europe through his writings), Paracelsus, Nicholas Flarnmel, John Frederick Helvetius, Raymond Lully, Alexander Sethon, Michael Sendivogius, Count Bernard of Treviso, Sir George Ripley, Picus de Mirandola, John Dee, Henry Khunrath, Michael Maier, Thomas Vaughan, J. B. von Helmont, John Heydon, Lascaris, Thomas Charnock, Synesius (Bishop of Ptolemais), Morieu, the Comte di Cagliostro, and the Comte de St.-Germain. There are legends to the effect that King Solomon and Pythagoras were alchemists and that the former manufactured by alchemical means the gold used in his temple.

"Albert Pike takes sides with the alchemical philosophers by declaring that the gold of the Hermetists was a reality. He says: "The Hermetic science, like all the real sciences, is mathematically demonstrable. Its results, even material, are as rigorous as that of a correct equation. The Hermetic Gold is not only a true dogma, a light without Shadow, a Truth without alloy of falsehood; it is also a material gold, real, pure, the most precious that can be found in the mines of the earth."

My father was a career military man who retired as a full Colonel from the Army. I grew up living on an Army base and actually joined Freemasonry still living on that base. When my father retired, he wanted to do something that he enjoyed, made him feel creative and relaxed him. He did something unexpected; he became a jeweler. He enjoyed creating pieces of jewelry. One day I was talking with my dad (a Freemason and Rosicrucian) about alchemy. He started laughing and asked, "When any jeweler creates a new piece of gold jewelry, do you *really* think that they use a piece of real gold to work on and take the chance of destroying something that expensive?" He pointed out that artificial gold is always used to practice on as the cost is far, far less and the look and feel is just like real gold. He also noted that just like artificial gold exists, so does artificial gems which are "grown" and even sold as such - one of the most popular being cubic zirconia which has the look and feel of real diamonds. It's not "booga booga nonsense;" it's what is common practice all over the world and is a large part of the jewelry business. It is also a fact that if a piece of artificial gold or an artificial gem were put in your hand, most people would have no idea that it was fake. In many cases, it would take a trained jeweler with expensive, modern equipment to determine the real from the fake.

Is it possible to make *real* gold from a base metal? I've never done it. But, it is very possible to make something that *looks, feels* and *seems* like real gold. It's done all the time. So, if you were to go back in time to when the alchemists were the "nutty old men in long robes" and they handed you (or some king) something that looked like, felt like, and by every known standard of the time *was* gold, what would be the conclusion? Is alchemy real?

But, was the true goal of alchemy ever to simply change base metals into gold and con noblemen out of their wealth? Could there be something more? Alchemy brings about a change. It claims to takes something less and it makes it of greater value. What does Freemasonry do? Do we claim to take good men and make them better? Is that a change and an improvement? Isn't that alchemy?

The alchemical process is a complex series of events with the goal of improving the nature of something - making it of more value. A moral, upright, educated man is viewed as of more value to society than a rogue. Freemasonry was originally designed to be a complex series of events (initiations and teachings) with the goal of taking someone basically good and helping them to become a better human being. The degrees of Freemasonry can be viewed as the alchemical steps. By comparing the rituals (any rite) and looking at the various old alchemical texts, we can see very similar core steps or instructions. We can see that it is very reasonable that one "borrowed" from the other. The concepts and basic goals of both alchemy and Freemasonry are too similar to discount some association and basic connection in the formative time of our Craft.

In the Star Wars movie, "The Empire Strikes Back", the young Jedi, Luke, unsuccessfully attempted to lift his X-wing fighter from a swamp. After several attempts, he gave up. He told the Jedi Master Yoda that lifting the fighter was impossible with the force as Yoda asked him to do. Yoda, before lifting the X-wing out of the swamp himself, told Luke: "You must unlearn what you have learned." There is a profound wisdom in that statement. There are times when many of us hold onto ideas, concepts or beliefs that deny us the opportunity of living a fuller, richer life.

As a boy, a good friend of mine had an older brother who was the source of all good information for us. He was older and far more experienced than us. We would be foolish not to listen to him. One day I remember going to an ice cream shop with my friend, his older brother and a few others. One of us started to order strawberry ice cream. The older boy jumped in saying that strawberry was the *worst* flavor made. He said that he would *never* eat it and anyone who did would be doing so at their own risk. That was enough for me. I never touched the stuff until I was an adult. Even then, it was only because I was in an awkward situation. I was invited over to a friend's house for dinner. After dinner, his wife brought in the dessert - homemade strawberry ice cream. I was uneasy as I knew it would taste horrible, but, I *had* to eat it or risk insulting them. To my amazement, it was wonderful! All through my childhood and for years into my adulthood, I denied myself something very good because I accepted something untested as a fact. I had to "unlearn" what I had learned about strawberry ice cream. What I also learned later on was that there was a reason why this older boy had such feelings about this flavor of ice cream. It turns out that he had a severe allergy to strawberries. It was not that he disliked the taste of it, but that strawberries did bad things to him.

Luke was his own worst enemy because of his early teachings. I was my own worst enemy because of what I believed. We all need to test what we know as "fact" and explore the possibilities that new truths might be waiting for us when we open up to them. Freemasonry may be more than a club. Our rituals may be more than just moral plays. And, alchemy may be something we wish to explore a little deeper.

"Do, or do not. There is no try." ~ Yoda

Freemasons and Rosicrucians

"Of all the theories which have been advanced in relation to the origin of Freemasonry from some one of the secret sects, either of antiquity or of the Middle Ages, there is none more interesting than that which seeks to connect it with the Hermetic philosophy, because there is none which presents more plausible claims to our consideration."

~ Albert G. Mackey

There is a thought that either one has always been a Rosicrucian, or he never will be one. I believe the same is true of Freemasonry. But, what does that mean? We are told that we are first made a Mason in our heart. What can that mean?

Some believe that who we are in the deepest reaches of our heart (soul, spirit, being) defines us and has always been of that nature, unchanged. With that, the deepest qualities of what it means to be a Freemason or a Rosicrucian have always been with us (or not) and membership only affords us the opportunity to explore the organizational philosophy in a setting, maybe, better suited for our personal advancement. I happen to be one who shares in such a belief.

My dog responds to her name. I can speak many other words, but there is no reaction in her. When I say her name, she responds. If I spoke my dog's name to another dog, there would probably be no response. There is nothing wrong with a dog that did not respond to my dog's name any more than there is anything wrong with my dog for not responding to another dog's name. All respond to what is familiar to them. There is nothing wrong with a philosophy reaching deep into one, yet not another. We all have different paths. The only problem comes when we pretend that something is reached by us when it is not. This often leads to changing what is not understood by us into something understandable. If you do not understand the use of a pen and you drive it into a wall like a nail, then you have denied yourself the true use and benefit of a pen. For you, its use has changed and becomes limited, and, not even as effective as a nail. An even greater danger than not knowing something is when it is coupled with the arrogant assumption that we "know it all."

I also happen to believe that, for me, there is a deep connection and tie between Rosicrucianism and Freemasonry. I believe that the connection is through the various initiations.

In his "Rosicrucian and Masonic Origins" Manly P. Hall writes:

"Freemasonry is a fraternity within a fraternity-an outer organization concealing an inner brotherhood of the elect. Before it is possible to intelligently discuss the origin of the Craft, it is necessary, therefore, to establish the existence of these two separate yet interdependent orders, the one visible and the other invisible. The visible society is a splendid camaraderie of "free and accepted" men enjoined to devote themselves to ethical, educational, fraternal, patriotic, and humanitarian concerns. The invisible society is a secret and most august fraternity whose members are dedicated to the service of a mysterious arcanum arcanorum. Those Brethren who have essayed to write the history of their Craft have not included in their disquisitions the story of that truly secret inner society which is to the body Freemasonic what the heart is to the body human. In each generation only a few are accepted into the inner sanctuary of the Work, but these are veritable Princes of the Truth and their sainted names shall be remembered in future ages together with the seers and prophets of the elder world. Though the great initiate-philosophers of Freemasonry can be counted upon one's fingers, yet their power is not to be measured by the achievements of ordinary men. They are dwellers upon the Threshold of the Innermost, Masters of that secret doctrine which forms the invisible foundation of every great theological and rational institution."

Why do we have initiations? Do we employ them for the benefit of the members watching the "plays" or do they have a deeper importance for the candidates?

There is a thought that for an initiation (Masonic, Rosicrucian or any other) to be of true value to the candidate there must be the proper setting, a desire to initiate and a desire to be initiated. A lacking in any of these elements may well result in a failed initiation. The words and floor work may be all correct and the initiation completely "legal" in the eyes of the Grand Lodge, but that special *something* which sometimes touches a candidate deep within may be missing. That *something* is what sets us apart from clubs and worthy charitable associations. It's what makes us a part of the ancient Mystery Schools and associates us with other mystical orders.

Proper initiation is thought to open *doors* for us. We may think of this in the physical sense and think of an actual door opening up and allowing us entrance into another room of a building. We may also think of this *building* as something much larger and not physical. The *door* that leads us to this other room may be thought of as the initiation itself.

A proper initiation assists us in traveling from one level (*room*) to another, to bring us places and afford us the opportunity for continued development or enlightenment. In all cases, it is our choice to accept and travel on, reject and remain in place or return to where we were. Each travels their own path. Each develops as they are guided. One path may be wholly unsuitable for one while a perfect fit for another. We should try to refrain from judgments regarding path choices. Zen philosophy teaches, "No snowflake ever falls in the wrong place."

The Rosicrucians are a *room* that a *door* may open for us. It is a path on the continuing journey towards self-development. It is a mistake to believe that Rosicrucianism (any more than Freemasonry) is a social club or a reward to be bestowed on those deemed popular, worthy or useful. You can not give something to one who already has it, or, will never have it. You can not *become* a Rosicrucian or have it taken away from you. You can only associate with others of like mind.

A proper initiation may make you aware of who and what you are. The opening of a door may allow you to feel things long forgotten, or it may only take you to an empty place of no use to you. We are who we are and it is only by expanding ourselves do we learn our path.

The Rosicrucians are tied to Freemasons just as one road leads to another in a journey. Even if we all end our journey at the same destination, there is no requirement to all travel on the same path. For some Rosicrucians and some Freemasons, the path is too similar to ignore and they recognize the mystic tie. Being a Rosicrucian is, for some, the same in their deepest being as being a Freemason. This path may have no meaning whatsoever to another. There is no gain in one path or loss in another.

Also in "Rosicrucian and Masonic Origins," Manly Hall writes:

"A new day is dawning for Freemasonry. From the insufficiency of theology and the hopelessness of materialism, men are turning to seek the God of philosophy. In this new era wherein the old order of things is breaking down and the individual is rising triumphant above the monotony of the masses, there is much work to be accomplished. The "Temple Builder" is needed as never before. A great reconstruction period is at hand; the debris of a fallen culture must be cleared away; the old footings must be found again that a new Temple significant of a new revelation of Law may be raised thereon. This is the peculiar work of the Builder; this is the high duty for which he was called out of the world; this is the noble enterprise for which he was "raised" and given the tools of his Craft. By thus doing his part in the reorganization of society, the workman may earn his "wages" as all good Masons should. A new light is breaking in the East, a more glorious day is at hand. The rule of the philosophic elect-the dream of the ages-will yet be realized and is not far distant. To her loyal sons, Freemasonry sends this clarion call: "Arise ye, the day of labor is at band; the Great Work awaits completion, and the days of man's life are few." Like the singing guildsman of bygone days, the Craft of the Builders marches victoriously down the broad avenues of Time. Their song is of labor and glorious endeavor; their anthem is of toil and industry; they rejoice in their noble destiny, for they are the Builders of cities, the Hewers of worlds, the Master Craftsmen of the universe!"

"Who looks outside, dreams; who looks inside, awakes." ~ Carl Gustav Jung

Guarding the West Gate

"Whence came the idea that a man - almost any man - has an inherent right to become a Freemason? Is it not a privilege to be conferred upon the worthy?"
~ Dwight L. Smith

We have earlier talked of the dangers faced by the medieval esoteric groups who gathered together in secret. The punishment for such gatherings and exploring of "unacceptable" subjects could be death. But, that was then and this is now. We live in much different times and can not be punished for gathering with like minded individuals for the study of obscure, or, even, unpopular scientific, philosophical or esoteric subjects. We have freedoms that did not exist in the medieval times. So, should this mean that we do not need to have any concern as to who joins us? Should we open the doors to anyone with any sort of interest? Such thoughts might display a misunderstanding of our nature and purpose.

Freemasonry exists today, in most parts of the world, in an atmosphere where our members do not fear for their lives simply for being a Freemason. A free society is one that does not proscribe membership in organizations promoting morality and free thought. But, we should not confuse the goal of the medieval esoteric societies and modern Freemasonry. The reason for limiting memberships in the esoteric societies was because not everyone was suited for the study of such subjects *and* for security concerns. While security is not normally an issue for Freemasonry today, it is still a fact that not everyone is suited for Freemasonry.

We may think of Freemasonry as a fine community orchestra. Many may like the music performed by the orchestra and there may be many applications to join the orchestra. But, not everyone is a musician. If the orchestra allowed anyone with an interest to join, regardless of their ability, or, inability, to play beautiful music, then the quality of the music would diminish greatly and so would the attendance wherever the orchestra performed. Before long the orchestra would cease to exist.

Freemasonry does not explicitly define *morality* or *worthy* but we do say that we only admit the *worthy* and are designed to make *good* men better. We investigate candidates wishing to join and vote on their *worthiness* to join us. Or, are we blowing smoke to make ourselves sound impressive and do we mean what we say? Do we understand what morality and worthy means in connection to Masonic membership?

If Freemasonry is an organization designed only for the moral and worthy, and if we knowingly, or because of careless investigation, admit the immoral or unworthy, Freemasonry, just like the fine community orchestra, will diminish in quality. Either we are what we claim or we are not. Just because Freemasonry was something at one time, does not mean that it will remain so regardless of what we do or how we act.

When we joined there were those who voted on us. In time, they went to their reward and we became the ones with the responsibility of the vote. We have a responsibility to the generations before us and an obligation to do what is in the best interest of Freemasonry.

The lodge investigation committee has the responsibility of determining the fitness of a candidate for Masonic membership. It should be assumed that the first "line of defense" of the lodge is the one who signs the petition. How well did he know the candidate? Is he a responsible brother who well knows the laws of Freemasonry? By the time the petition gets to the investigation committee, (in most cases) the lodge has already voted on receiving the petition. They have shown some interest in the candidate and accept the statements given and pass on the petition to the investigation committee for detailed study.

The system fails if the first real investigation of a candidate is when the petition is given to an investigation committee. *All* must do their part to insure that none but "fine musicians" are admitted to our Masonic "orchestra." No petition should reach an investigation committee if anyone has any doubts about the candidate.

If we carefully consider the duties of the Investigation Committee, we can begin to see its awesome responsibility. The Investigation Committee is asked to investigate and pass judgment on the fitness for membership of another human being, and that would include the moral fitness. No considerate individual will fail to recognize the enormous responsibility being given this committee. In my opinion, there is no committee that has a more profound responsibility than the Investigation Committee. The proper performance of this committee is not only vitally important to your Lodge, but to the whole of Masonry.

Your Lodge or Grand Lodge may provide instructions on the composition of the Investigation Committee. Many jurisdictions provide for a three member committee with a Past Master serving as the Chairman. Regardless of the composition, this committee, like others, best operates with a plan to follow. When the Worshipful Master appoints the committee, they should set a time to meet as soon as possible so that they can begin their work. The Investigation Committee should first completely examine all available information provided on the petition. The last thing a Lodge needs is to learn of misstatements on a petition after a petitioner has received the three degrees. The committee should then begin the task of systematically investigating all aspects of the character of the petitioner. It is incorrect to think that a comprehensive investigation is an unwarranted intrusion into the privacy of the petitioner. When one seeks to join Freemasonry, then Freemasonry must determine if he is worthy.

Over the last few years there has been a trend developing in a number of jurisdictions. Not only has there been a growing desire for new members, but an almost hunger or fervor for new members. It is not difficult to imagine that such strong desire for new candidates might adversely affect the careful consideration of each petition. If even the impression is given that the goal is merely more members, as that of a club membership drive, then an investigation committee could be viewed as more of a formality which can operate in something of a "rubber stamp" approval process. Investigations might be limited to verifying the names and addresses. That sort of practice is contrary to our teachings and detrimental to all of Freemasonry. Masonry does not need more members, Masonry needs more Masons. If we do not see the difference, then we are dooming ourselves to a slow (or quick) corruption of all for which we have stood since our creation.

It would seem that if we fail to understand the nature of something, it can often be confused with something else leading to disastrous results. If we think of the general category of food, we can add both fish and apples to that group. If we think of the nature of a fish being the same as the nature of an apple, then we have made a serious error. They are not the same thing. Masonry can be included in a general category with many fine organizations. Specifically, however, Masonry does not operate like the Red Cross, Salvation Army, Lions Club or as any other service or charitable organization. Likewise, Masonry is not a religion and does not operate as such. We do not offer salvation or promises of aid to any and all who knock on our door. While it is true that we can often see individual Masons offering service to communities, that is not our primary goal.

Masonry has a very specific task and that is self-improvement. The reason why Past Masters are often required to be the chairman of investigation committees is because it is assumed that by the time one has become a Past Master, he should well know the exact purpose of Masonry. The experienced Past Master can lead the other members of the committee to recognizing if the petitioner is a proper fit for Masonry.

The Investigation Committee must also not be confused when we say that Masonry is a moral institution. Masonry is for the morally fit, but it is not an "either/or" situation. If one is rejected for membership, it does not automatically mean that we are judging them as morally unfit. Being moral is a requirement for Masonic membership, but not every moral person is a proper candidate for Masonry. For example, if the wife of a petitioner objects to her husband becoming a Mason, then he should be rejected for membership. In this case, the man might be wholly upright and moral, but Masonry must not interfere with family harmony. If the petitioner is married, his wife must support his initiation. If he is single and lives at home, then his parents must support his becoming a Mason. There are many valid reasons for rejecting a candidate that have nothing to do with morality.

Another area of confusion is with religion and politics. Masons know that these are taboo subjects when a Lodge is at labor. Wise Masons also avoid pointed discussions or debates of these subjects even when the Lodge is not at labor. The reason should be obvious. We all have our political opinions and religious beliefs. We recognize and respect that our faiths and opinions may differ and we also recognize that pointed discussions of these subjects might cause disharmony. But how does this affect an Investigation Committee?

Well, being respectful of the various religious beliefs or political opinions does not mean that we do not know how our brothers feel or believe. We should know each other and still respect each other as brothers. I have heard some say that all questions concerning religion and politics should be avoided with a petitioner; that only the questions, "Do you believe in a Supreme Being?" and "Are you a citizen of this country?" should be asked. I very much disagree with this line of thinking. It was stated to me that one reason why it was believed that no discussion of religion or politics should be permitted when interviewing a petitioner was in case any member of the investigation committee held biases against any particular religious faith or political party. What an incredible way of thinking! Such thinking automatically assumes that we have unworthy individuals on our committees who will evaluate petitioners in an unMasonic manner! We should stop and consider this aspect with a bit of clear thinking.

We call our members "Brother" and this should give us a clue as to how we should view our fellow Masons. We are members of the Masonic *family*. We need only to think of our Obligations to realize the relationship that should exist between Masons. The Investigation Committee is not only to investigate the character of the petitioner and his fitness for Masonry, but is also a "get to know" committee. The members of the committee should try to learn about this individual who may soon be their brother and give the petitioner a chance to get to know the committee members. If our only interest is in the money given for the degrees, then maybe we would not care that much about getting to know the petitioner. If we are, however, investigating an individual who we might for the rest of our lives call "brother," then we should want to get to know all about this individual.

But does Masonry enter into the realm of religion and politics? Do we evaluate and pass judgment on religions and political parties? No. Religions and political parties are not eligible to join Masonry. Masonry admits and investigates *individuals*. Should you ask a petitioner to which religion he belongs? Is it improper to even ask such a question? No, it's not. If we do not ask pointed questions, how will we learn what should be learned? Would you welcome into your lodge one who is a member of the Nazi Party or the Church of Satan? One member of an investigation committee told me that this is exactly what happened once when he served on this committee. A petitioner seemed very normal, stated that he did believe in a Supreme Being and during a normal conversation, the question of to which religion he belonged came up. Without hesitation he stated that he was a member of the Church of Satan and then went on to show the committee his "ceremony room" filled with satanic paraphernalia.

The brother said that had they not asked him this simple question, he would likely have been voted into the lodge as all else about him seemed normal - from what they could tell.

At some point, common sense must be employed. If the nature or actions of an individual are out of line with Masonry and considered immoral to reasonable people, should we allow such an individual to join Masonry because he belongs to a religion or political party that condones such activity? No, we should not.

In our world today, the term "politically correct" often dictates what some feel is and is not proper. We will find cases today where some will argue that it is not proper to investigate someone beyond verifying their name and address. We will find some who object to the idea of any sort of investigation of a petitioner. Make no mistake, these "politically correct" opinions do not serve Masonry. Freemasonry was never designed to be open to any and all. It is impossible to get into the closed heart or mind of a petitioner to know their deepest secrets. No investigation committee can guarantee that an unworthy individual will not gain admission to our Lodges, but we must try. We must conduct our investigations in as diligent and fair a manner as possible. We must put the well-being of the Lodge and the whole of Masonry in the forefront of our decisions and use the teachings of Masonry as our guide.

Unfortunately, there is no book that will provide the correct answers to every possible scenario that an investigation committee can face. The members of this committee must be able to think on their feet. They must be able to take the teachings of Freemasonry and apply them to each situation they encounter. A petitioner must not be excluded for petty, external reasons, but they also must not be accepted for fear of not seeming "politically correct." We should look only at the internal qualities of the petitioner and determine if he is a good match for our Lodge. Masonry is designed to make the good, better, not to make the unacceptable, acceptable. We are not a reform school, nor are we a place that is designed to bring trouble into a family, nor a club that accepts any and all with the proper payment.

Guarding the West Gate means that we must welcome the worthy and keep out the unworthy. The Investigation Committee is to use their good common sense, diligent efforts and the pure teachings of Masonry to attempt the task of guarding this most important gate.

"The truth is incontrovertible. Malice may attack it, ignorance may deride it, but in the end, there it is." ~ Winston Churchill

Where is Freemasonry Going?

"When it comes to the future, there are three kinds of people: those who let it happen, those who make it happen, and those who wonder what happened."
~ John M. Richardson, Jr.

We have all read or heard stories of individuals who have taken drastic steps to save their own lives. Recently I read of a man who was doing some repair work on his water heater. He needed to reach far into the tank while lying on his back. While working in that position, his arm became wedged in the tank and he found that it was impossible to remove it. He screamed for help, but was alone in the house and no one was near enough outside to hear his cries. The man had spent several days trapped with his arm hopelessly wedged when he noticed a disturbing smell coming from inside the tank and around his arm. The man later recounted that instinct must have taken over. He managed to reach a saw and began to cut off his arm. The next day, several family members - concerned at not being able to reach him - found him unconscious on the floor in a pool of blood, his arm severed at the elbow. The man was taken to the hospital where he recovered, but the doctors gave him a sobering report. Gangrene had set into his arm, and he was told that if he had not removed it when he did, he would have died. The doctors also noted that if he had waited any longer to remove the arm, it would have been too late. The poison would have spread through his body and nothing then would have saved him. The man's life was saved not just because he took action, but when he took action.

I joined Masonry in the mid-'70s. While a number of my family members had been Masons, I knew next to nothing of the philosophy or history of Freemasonry. All that I knew was that it was a "good" organization. It took my joining to find out what "good" meant. Such ignorance of the philosophy of Freemasonry prior to joining is becoming more of the exception than the rule today. Many of the young men who join Masonry already know much of its philosophy. They have read the popular, new and exciting books on Freemasonry. They arrive at the door of the Lodge with an awareness of a wonderful, mysterious, moral and enlightened group of seekers. They want to share in and be a part of such an organization. But, sadly, this is not exactly what they always find when they join.

The numbers of demits, NPD, and non-participation are growing at an alarming rate. The new reports paint a dismal picture. Yes, new members are coming fast, and sometimes in very good numbers, but we seem to be having trouble keeping them. So, why is this happening and what do we do?

What seems to be happening is the young men come to Freemasonry with an idea of what it should be and find that it is something very different. Many come with the hopes of finding enlightening discussions, intellectual programs designed to lift us to new heights and help us learn more of ourselves and our world. Yet, sometimes all they find is "good ole boys" seeking to add another title, gain a bit more authority or power, and be more of the "big fish" in whatever pond they thrive. There is lots of coffee, but little real enlightenment. The young Masons become upset at the reality of their Masonry when they compare it to what they believed of Masonry before they joined. Some make their displeasure known - loudly. At times, such pointed objections by the young brothers are met with disapproval. It is perceived that the young Masons know nothing of what they are talking, are out of place, need to "get with the program" and stop "being so negative." The upset young Masons are viewed as the troublemakers and their cries for Masonry as they believe it should be are viewed more as the cries of malcontents. They are often ignored and sometimes ostracized. The Masons become disillusioned and wonder why they ever joined.

What happens next takes us back to the man with his arm wedged in the tank of the water heater. At the moment he began to smell something very bad, he had a choice. He could act or he could wait and see. Acting in a decisive manner saved his life; waiting to see if the situation changed on its own would have cost him his life. As in many cases, timing is everything. In Freemasonry, our gangrene is apathy. If apathy towards Freemasonry, or any body of Freemasonry, sets into anyone then they stop caring. Once they stop caring, Masonry does not matter to them and they turn their back, demit, stop paying their dues or just live as a card carrier. The positive force that could have been dies. We all lose.

And, whose fault is it if a Mason stops caring about Masonry? If we believe or say that it is in some way the fault of the disillusioned Mason, that he would "do better to bring about changes on the inside" or some other such criticism designed to shame him into remaining a member, then we add insult to injury. We have missed the point and are only making a bad situation worse. It would be the same as if we saw the man with his arm wedged in the tank and we advised him to be patient and hang on a bit longer as things will certainly get better if he just waits out the unpleasant situation. When does "hanging on" reach the point of gangrene and result in death no matter what is done after?

In all cases, objectivity, recognition of the actual situation and the courage to do what needs to be done must be paramount. If a dedicated, serious Mason ceases to care about some Masonic body, then the "blame game" of identifying who is at fault is pointless. Apathy has won and Masonry loses.

The time to act is when we see the first signs of actual trouble. The first thing the man with his arm wedged did was try to free his arm. He twisted it, moved it this way and that and did everything he could do to free it. This is the same as if we belong to a dysfunctional Masonic body and we try to suggest ways to improve the body, work for changes and do all we can to correct the situation as a member. If nothing works, then we must take the next step.

When all his own efforts could not free his arm, the man began yelling for help. He was clearly not in a position to effect any positive change in the situation; maybe someone else could render him aid. In Masonry, the calling for help would come in the form of seeking out superiors who might be able to correct the situation. When our own best efforts fail, and they sometimes do, we need to seek help from those in a position who might be able to grant what we need.

And what do we do if no help comes? In all cases, we need to act responsibly. We can not act in haste, foolishly or without considered thought. But at some point we need to act. Failure to take any action is often just as reckless and foolish as an action taken too quickly. At some point, the man with his arm wedged knew that something was very wrong. He may not have known all the details or possessed all the medical knowledge of the situation, but he knew that he needed to take drastic action to correct the situation. Oh yes, help did arrive just the next day. But, it was too late. The doctors told him that if he had waited those additional hours, the poison would have gone through his body and then nothing would have been able to save him. He took the necessary action and he took it in time to save his life.

No one told us that being a Mason was always going to be easy. If someone did, they told us a story. Throughout our degrees, we are given lessons of honor, integrity and courage. We are given lessons that are sometimes very difficult to put into practice. In my Craft Masonry, we use the Scottish Rite Craft ritual. We are taught that the three "villains" in craft Masonry represent ignorance, falsehood and ambition. If we have a deficiency of the former or allow any of the later to gain hold of us, then we do not live Freemasonry as we were taught. Our goal is to control and advance ourselves. We must live our own lives as Masonry teaches us. We have no control over another, even our closest brother, but we must always have total control over ourselves.

Freemasonry is going through a revolution of sorts. Gone are the days of the "good ole boy" clubs, the power brokers or the joining of one organization only because it is viewed as a prerequisite for another organization. The young Masons come to us with an understanding of the value of what we teach, not the shiny trinkets we wear. The beauty of what is taught in the various bodies is desired. The leadership of every single body in Masonry must provide quality education, leadership and teach what is supposed to be learned by the new members. If it is in any way unclear as to what is supposed to be taught in any Masonic body, then that should give the clear signal that a change is in order in those bodies. When the ones who must teach don't know themselves, the whole body suffers. Stand up, do the work that you need to do or allow another to do the work.

Luckily, in many cases we find that only the first step is necessary in dysfunctional Masonic bodies. We are finding more and more cases of the new members realizing that something is very lacking, standing up and taking control of the lacking Lodges and making the positive changes themselves. In those bodies where the membership is not in a position to make such changes on their own authority, then assistance from superiors is necessary or the body will crumble. Period.

Apathy is the cancer we can not allow to set into any Mason. Our new, young Masons have a foundation that brings with them a hope for our future that is too valuable to ignore. We must do all in our power to see that their interest, dedication and hunger for Masonry is not trampled by the unworthy or their death grip on their perceived power.

We are in new wonderful times. We must always look to tomorrow if we have any hope of a future than includes Freemasonry. Where is Freemasonry going? It's following a path.

"As far as we can discern, the sole purpose of existence is to kindle a light in the darkness of being."

~ Carl Jung

Peace

www.ingramcontent.com/pod-product-compliance
Lightning Source LLC
Chambersburg PA
CBHW031512270326
41930CB00006B/371